D1613562

The Columbia Restaurant Spanish Cookbook

University Press of Florida

Florida A&M University, Tallahassee
Florida Atlantic University, Boca Raton
Florida Gulf Coast University, Ft. Myers
Florida International University, Miami
Florida State University, Tallahassee
New College of Florida, Sarasota
University of Central Florida, Orlando
University of Florida, Gainesville
University of North Florida, Jacksonville
University of South Florida, Tampa
University of West Florida, Pensacola

University Press of Florida

Gainesville • Tallahassee • Tampa
Boca Raton • Pensacola • Orlando
Miami • Jacksonville • Ft. Myers
Sarasota

THE
COLUMBIA
RESTAURANT
SPANISH COOKBOOK

Adela Hernandez Gonzmart
and Ferdie Pacheco

19 18 17 16 15   19 18 17 16 15 14

Library of Congress Cataloging-in-Publication Data
Gonzmart, Adela Hernandez.
The Columbia Restaurant Spanish cookbook / Adela Hernandez
Gonzmart and Ferdie Pacheco.
p. cm.
Includes index.
ISBN 978-0-8130-1403-6 (alk. paper)
1. Cookery, Spanish. 2. Columbia Restaurant—History.
I. Pacheco, Ferdie. II. Title.
TX723.5.S7G69 1995
641.5945—dc20   95-16806

The University Press of Florida is the scholarly publishing agency for the State University System of Florida, comprising Florida A&M University, Florida Atlantic University, Florida Gulf Coast University, Florida International University, Florida State University, New College of Florida, University of Central Florida, University of Florida, University of North Florida, University of South Florida, and University of West Florida.

University Press of Florida
15 Northwest 15th Street
Gainesville, FL 32611-2079
http://www.upf.com

I dedicate this book to my grandfather,
Casimiro Hernandez I, my father,
Casimiro Hernandez II, and my husband,
Cesar Gonzmart. These three men worked unselfishly
to make a dream come true and keep it alive.

—ADELA HERNANDEZ GONZMART

Contents

RECIPES IN ENGLISH

RECETAS EN ESPAÑOL

POLLO Y PAVO 171

SALSAS 199

$\mathcal{P}$ R E F A C E

From my earliest recollection of being taken to the Columbia Restaurant by my Aunt Lola to eat a delicious Cuban sandwich, I have always associated Adela Hernandez Gonzmart with the glittering world of the Columbia, a neighborhood gathering place in the Cuban-Spanish-Italian community of Ybor City, Florida.

My life has interwoven with hers. She was a few years older, and the idealization of what I thought was a perfect girl. To my young eyes, she was beautiful, impossibly talented, famous, popular, witty and personable, and, most of all, inaccessible.

Our families were very close. Her father and uncle owned the restaurant, and her grandfather had started it. My Aunt Lola was the main cashier at the restaurant until she died, and as a teenager I worked as a waiter in the coffee shop, in the kitchen, and behind the bar.

So this cookbook is a distillate of my lifelong admiration of and friendship with Adela and her family.

When we first decided to write this book I thought it would be a fairly simple task. After all, I had completed a rather thorough research of the Columbia Restaurant for a chapter in my book *Ybor City Chronicles*, and Adela had a full file of recipes of the dishes that made the restaurant a highly successful establishment for ninety years.

But when my wife, Luisita, and I sat down at Adela's house to work, we found a mountain of material to sort through. Cases upon cases of wonderful old photographs presented themselves. Adela's memory was sharp, and she came up with interesting anecdotes about her life. After all, the book was to be the story of Adela and the romance of the Columbia.

In order to present the publisher with an organized, readable manuscript, Adela and I needed an editor who could type, write, and push us to drain our cup of stories, recipes, and photos. We were lucky to have Luisita, who volunteered her services. While studying flamenco dancing in Sevilla in the 1960s, Luisita acquired a love for Andalusian cooking. In addition to her knowledge of Hispanic cuisine, she brought to this project the brain of an editor, the heart and discipline of an entertainer, and the back of a stevedore. With our deadline pressing us, she chained herself to the word processor and did not get up until the work was done.

As a member of the family of the Columbia from my youth, and having worked there in its golden years, I must acknowledge the cast of the Columbia Restaurant. From their lifelong contributions and from the thousands of stories they told me, the text of this book was written.

The bulk of the book is comprised of the contributions of the proprietors, Casimiro and Lawrence Hernandez, and Adela, Cesar, Richard, and Casey Gonzmart.

The customers past and present (many of them famous in Ybor) who had hunkered down to have coffee twenty times a day were the source of many important insights.

The Italian customers included produce dealers J. C. Valenti, Tony Valenti, the Lazzaras, the Pardos, and the Geracis; Santo Trafficante, father and son, kingpins of the world of bolita (the numbers game), and their shadow, Jimmy Longo; Chicken Cacciatore, the bolita man at the café; and the banker and head of the Draft Board, Anthony Grimaldi.

Customers who were political cronies of Lawrence included Frank Alonso, a brilliant raconteur; Manuel Garcia, our best lawyer; and my father, J.B., who never missed a day at the Columbia.

Two dentists, as different as day from night, frequented the Columbia: one-armed Dr. Rex Myers and the politician Dr. Vic Rosenthal, a tough but funny man.

The architect Ivo de Minicis and the builder Domingo Rañon, with their knowledge of Italian and Spanish Mediterranean architecture, contributed so much to creating the look and ambience of the Quixote, Patio, and Siboney rooms, where they then became regular customers.

Also among the restaurant's regulars were the zanies: Pan con Chinches, the resident charity case; Pepe Lu Babo, the babbling newsboy; and Crazy Benny, who carried a rubber briefcase.

And in the midst of all the hubbub one customer stood out for his composure, dignity, quiet wit, intelligence, and extraordinary kindness and charity. Cesar Medina, of Holsum Bakeries, had such clarity of vision and such admired principles that his advice and help were sought out by everyone.

The lifelong employees contributed much to the anecdotal material, but since they merit a chapter in the book I will only list them here: Pijuan, the chef; Pete, the bartender; Pepin, the headwaiter; El Rey (Gregorio Martinez), king of the waiters; Henry Tudela, the master pianist; Sarapico, the second chef; and my Aunt Lola, the cashier.

Columbia's in-house photographer Fiol Cruz contributed his time in reproducing all the historical photographs that appear in the book. Luis Diaz contributed to the chapter on the wines of the Columbia.

For historical information I turned to Roland Manteiga, editor-publisher of *La Gaceta;* Hampton Dunn and Leland Hawes, the *Tampa Tribune* writers who have become deans of Tampa history; Gary Mormino, history professor at the University of South Florida; and Joe Guidry of the editorial staff of the *Tampa Tribune.*

Anyone writing about Ybor City must start at the source, and I was fortunate to mine the treasures of Tony Pizzo before he passed on. Tony Pizzo, like many in Ybor City, had a love affair with the Columbia Restaurant, and his was a detailed and well-annotated contribution to the book.

Phil LoCicero gave a detailed account of an Italian Christmas Eve.

The final and biggest acknowledgment goes to a man who passed away many years ago but whose work was a tremendous help to us in writing this book. Paul Wilder was a *Tampa Tribune* writer, reporter, and columnist for many years. When he needed a side job he discovered that the Columbia Restaurant could use a column to appear in lieu of advertisement. For several years Wilder collected anecdotes, reported unusual happenings, and printed recipes. He was the Boswell of the Columbia Restaurant.

Serendipity was with us when Adela unearthed three volumes of Wilder's work, which had been collected by Edith Smith Carryl and was given to Adela with fond memories for many enjoyable meals eaten at the Columbia. We were twice-blessed when we found photographs that illustrated the story, including a priceless photo of Pepin the headwaiter, a prize-winning cow the Columbia had bought, and Pijuan, with a cleaver in hand ready to start work.

For me, along with the chance to produce a history and cookbook of the Columbia Restaurant came the bigger opportunity to capture the remarkable life of the vibrant, multifaceted Adela Hernandez Gonzmart. Working with Adela, the Princess Grace of Ybor City, proved to me that she had not lost the charm, wit, intelligence, memory, and storytelling ability I remembered as a youth. Her training as a concert pianist is still evident. She is a disciplined worker, a perfectionist, impatient to get things right, and driven to record her journey accurately for posterity. In her I can see her father's grim work ethic and her mother Carmita's great good humor and conviviality.

Given the clarity with which Adela recalled the events of her life, I decided that whenever possible her voice should be represented in the first person. The writing style that evolved was one in which my voice became the straight narrative line and Adela interjected her voice where applicable. (Her portions of the dialogue appear in an italic typeface.) In the end, I became the straight man for her punch lines. I believe in this way we both tell our story and also capture the charismatic qualities of this remarkable woman.

This collaboration between old friends proved to be the happiest of events, and allowed us to share the fun and reward of reviewing the ninety-year history of a great old establishment, the Columbia Restaurant, the Gem of All Spanish Restaurants.

—FERDIE PACHECO

I have known Ferdie Pacheco all his life. His father, Baltasar, was one of my father's best friends. I was always impressed by his father's intelligence, by his knowledge of music, and by his name. He was named after one of the three wise men who brought gifts to Jesus Christ when He was born.

Just about the time that Ferdie was born, I began my musical studies with Pennsylvania Pacheco, Baltasar's stepmother. She lived only two blocks from Ferdie's parents' home, and my mother would often visit Ferdie's mother after my piano lesson. Ferdie was always getting into some kind of mischief, while his older brother was completely the opposite, always involved with his books and artistic endeavors. Little did we know that Fernandito, as we used to call him then, would become what we all know him to be today: an artist, a writer, a doctor, and a world-renowned expert on boxing. But above all, he is an unusual human being. He loves people from many different walks of life, he helps the needy, and he never forgets his old friends.

The years have gone by, and both of us have had our ups and downs, but Ferdie and I have always had one strong bond: love for the Columbia. If it were not for Ferdie's enthusiasm and persistence, this book would not have been written. It is truly a love story, encompassing love of family, love of country, love of community, and love of one's fellow man.

Thank you, Ferdie, for making this work of love a reality.

—ADELA HERNANDEZ GONZMART

Chapter One

The Spanish-Cuban Heritage of Florida Cooking

The quincentennial celebration of the Columbus voyage caused many of us to reflect on the pivotal event of the past five hundred years. Columbus's discovery of the New World had tremendous global impact on many aspects of life, including food. Since then, food has shaped cultures and determined destinies.

Chocolate, vanilla, corn, chilies, peanuts, tomatoes, avocados, squashes, beans (both dried and green), sweet potatoes, potatoes, pineapples, papayas, and guavas, to name the most significant, went from the New World back to the Old. Had the expeditions into the New World not been so inspired by food—pepper and other spices (often used to preserve food) in particular—less attention might have been paid to the food that was found.

The mostly meatless New World expanded its diet with pigs, cattle, chickens, oil, wine, citrus, cinnamon, cloves, rice, wheat, peaches, apricots, milk, butter, and sugar. The horse brought mobility; oxen and mules brought better ways to work the land.

Spain, just free of centuries of Arab domination, had embraced culinary contributions from Europe, Asia, and the Arab countries and in turn brought those to the New World. On the Spanish-speaking islands, dish after dish be-

gins with *sofrito,* a sauté of chopped onions, green peppers, garlic, and tomatoes. Meat, fish, and fowl usually are marinated with herbs (especially oregano and bay leaf), garlic, and lemon, lime, or sour orange juice.

Another great influence on Caribbean cooking was the influx of African
slaves, who utilized okra (Cubans still call it by its African name, *quimbombó*),
malanga, and other tropical fruits.

In the early 1800s, agitation against the slave system began to surface in
Europe, and plantation owners found they needed a new labor force. Their
solution was to import large numbers of servants from the Orient, who introduced rice to the Caribbean plate. A Cuban meal is hardly ever complete
without white rice as an accompaniment.

It is the interplay of aboriginal, European, African, and Oriental influences
that has given Caribbean cuisines their shape.

An Arawak Indian *barbacoa* (barbecue)—a "grate" of thin green stalks upon
which meat was grilled above an open fire—came to be important in the Caribbean. To this day, all Spanish-speaking countries use the word *barbacoa* for
this method of cooking.

Although the plantain, cousin of the banana, is really a fruit, it must be
cooked to be palatable and so is usually thought of as a vegetable. The plantain reached southern Europe via Africa in the caravans of Arab traders, who
had discovered it growing in India. Plantain shoots were brought to the Caribbean islands by the Spaniards, but it is now believed that plantains already
grew on some islands when the Spanish arrived.

Plantains, though less sweet than bananas, are more versatile. They can be
cooked and eaten at various stages of ripeness, and each stage has its own taste
and treatment. Green plantains, which are almost as hard as potatoes, are delicious cut into slivers, fried, and served as chips. But it is when fully ripe that
the plantain is most glorious. It is usually cut in half-inch diagonal slices and
fried in oil, making it crisp outside and soft inside. Its mild but definite sweetness blends magnificently with pork or chicken, and it makes beef more interesting too.

Once it was apparent that there was a limit to the gold to be had from the
islands, the Spaniards, the earliest colonizers in the Caribbean, viewed their
new possessions as supply houses from which to feed the busy conquistadors

on the mainland. And so from the beginning of their settlement on Hispaniola they imported cattle, pigs, sheep, and horses from Spain. The Spaniards continued to maintain diversified farming on their islands, including Cuba and Puerto Rico; thus, to this day there are more beef dishes on the Spanish-speaking islands than on others. Many such dishes are Caribbean translations of recipes from Spain, but like all translations they take on characters of their own, differing from the originals in subtle but important ways. Cuba's popular *picadillo* is clearly descended from an old Moorish dish cooked with olives and raisins, but it also contains the New World prizes of tomatoes and peppers, which the modern Spanish have in turn adopted.

Lechón asado, whole spit-roasted young pig, is Cuba's traditional main course on Christmas Eve (Noche Buena). Spain has *cochinillo asado,* a very young roasted pig weighing about seven pounds, which influenced the Cuban interpretation of preparing a whole pig. The difference is that the Spanish version is more subtle, using less garlic and no spices. But sour orange is used in Spain, as in Cuba, for the marinade.

Many of the Spaniards who emigrated to Cuba came from the northern provinces of Asturias and Galicia. Because of the cold climate, hearty soups like *caldo gallego* and *fabada* are very popular there. When these Spaniards came to the New World, they used their familiar cooking methods but added many vegetables (roots, corn, beans) and spices that were unique to the New World. Corn chowder, called *guiso de maíz,* and *ajiaco,* a heavy soup made with pork, flank steak, jerk beef, malanga, yucca, sweet potatoes, corn on the cob, pumpkin, plantains, onions, green peppers, and tomatoes, were favorite new dishes. And, of course, black beans (*frijoles negros*), the heartiest and meatiest of beans, are traditionally served with snowy white rice and topped with chopped onions. The black and white combination of beans and rice cooked together is known colloquially as the Cuban dish *Moros y Cristianos* (Moors and Christians). Some Spaniard with a good sense of humor must have come up with this name.

In the late nineteenth century, a wave of immigrants mostly from Spain and Cuba came to Tampa, Florida. What started this emigration? The cigar industry.

In 1884 two unusual visitors arrived in Tampa. Bernardo Gargol, a Spanish purveyor of jellies and fruits in Cuba, and Gavino Gutierrez, a gifted Spanish civil engineer and businessman, had come in search of groves of mangos and guavas believed to exist on Florida's west coast. Disappointed by their failure to locate sources of guava paste, they were nonetheless impressed by what they saw. Returning by sea to New York, the Spaniards stopped over at Key West, where they called on their countryman, Vicente Martinez Ybor, a cigar manufacturer. Key West possessed no fresh water supply and could be reached only by sea, so Ybor was anxious to relocate his cigar industry.

Gutierrez told Ybor about Tampa's railroad and steamship facilities and the region's notorious humidity, which would create a natural humidor for tobacco leaf. Ybor moved to Tampa and in 1885 opened its first cigar factory. Many others who had left Spain for Cuba eventually moved to Martinez Ybor's experimental community. Soon, this section of Tampa became known as Ybor City. Thousands of Cubans and Spaniards left their countries upon hearing of the great opportunities that this growing settlement offered. Most of these immigrants were men, so boardinghouses and restaurants were needed. They were mostly owned by Spaniards, but in 1904, Casimiro Hernandez I came from Cuba to Ybor City and opened a small café.

Chapter Two

BREAKFAST

AT THE

COLUMBIA

FERDIE: Breakfast at the Columbia Café was a ritual for many Ybor City men, traveling salesmen, hunters, fishermen, and insomniacs. Initially, and for many years, the Columbia coffee shop was always open, twenty-four hours a day, seven days a week. It never closed.

Most men had two breakfasts. One at home taken hurriedly, amid the domestic turmoil of wife and children, and the other at their leisure, at the Columbia, in the company of friends and associates, and in the warmth of continuous camaraderie.

The breakfast most commonly ordered was simple and cheap. It consisted of *café con leche* (coffee with boiled milk) and toasted *pan Cubano con mantequilla* (Cuban bread and butter). For years this meal cost fifteen cents. If you wanted a larger cup, it was a dime more. The tip, if there was one—and in the hard times tips were unknown—was a nickel. I did receive a three-penny tip a few times, mostly from accountants, who can compute percentages accurately. I worked the breakfast-lunch shift as a young waiter at the café during World War II, and it was neither fun nor profitable.

People who habituated the old café always say to me, "The coffee is not the same as it was in those days."

ADELA: *My grandfather brought over a special blend of coffee beans, which*

5

he ground and roasted and used in the café. It was different from any other coffee in town.

My Uncle Gus was given the Columbia Coffee Mill to produce the coffee, and he ran it profitably until he tired of it and decided to open a bakery instead. At that time my other uncle, Evelio, the youngest son, was coming out of the army, and he inherited the mill.

When Evelio died in the 1980s, the mill closed. Then we ran into difficulties

The Columbia
Restaurant at night,
1950.

because we couldn't get coffee as good as we had been making. It was a big problem for a long time.

Finally I'd had enough, and I tracked down the old man who had worked with Evelio. He was working at the Naviera Coffee Mill on Seventh Avenue.

"Can you blend the coffee like you used to for Evelio?"

"Yes, I can," he answered, and he did mix the right proportions of different beans.

I went right home and boiled the coffee, put it through the sock-strainer, added sugar, and tasted it apprehensively.

*"Now this is like the coffee we **used** to have at the Columbia, great coffee," I said, smacking my lips and pouring a second cup with a smile on my face.*

FERDIE: Now milk was a different thing. It was boiled in the back in big five-gallon vats. Pinches of salt were added from time to time. When it was boiling, it was brought to the café and poured into a serving vat, which kept it hot. It was used up every hour, so it didn't get a chance to taste burned. The indispensable element in *café con leche* is freshness. Old reheated Cuban coffee tastes like butane lighter fluid. Old milk is a burnt mess that assaults the taste buds.

By virtue of the rapid turnover, the Columbia coffee was always fresh. By and large, that was the secret of Columbia coffee: freshness and a "secret" blend of beans. Columbia coffee. I'd pay a dollar for a cup. In fact, I just did.

Cuban bread and butter was another treat. It also had to be fresh, made that morning. People waited outside until they saw the bags of bread delivered from La Segunda Central Bakery. It was worth the wait.

It was the job of the sandwich maker to attend to the oven and the heating of the succulent bread. Customers had different tastes and demands, and they were very fussy. There were all kinds of different orders: Bread, not toasted, butter applied. Bread, end-cut, butter applied, toasted. Bread, either end-cut or mid-loaf, toasted, *then* butter applied. Old bread, yesterday's tips, for *sopitas,* which were bits of bread put in the cup, sugar sprinkled over the bits, with *café con leche* poured over it all.

Old, hard Cuban bread should never be thrown away. *Sopitas* are delicious, and if you like desserts, the bread can be used for bread pudding.

There were greedy customers who ordered the toast with a "once-over" or "one-way." This referred to how the pantryman applied the butter. The spatula usually went over the bread, leaving a thick layer of butter; then, going the other way, the excess was taken off. Customers who ordered a "one-way" (no excess removed) got a big load of butter on their bread.

ADELA: *The bread served in Spain is very hard, both the crust and inside. It's probably a delight for dentists, for it could break a tooth easily. The flour used in Spain is not as refined as the flour we have because it is not milled like ours. The bread I knew in Cuba was very light, of a much lighter consistency than we know in Tampa. Made mostly of flour and water with hardly any salt in it.*

*We should not call our bread Cuban bread (**pan Cubano**); we should call it Ybor City bread or Tampa bread.*

There's a funny thing about this bread. The bread we make at the restaurants in St. Augustine and elsewhere, using the same formula, turns out very different. To me, Ybor or Tampa bread is unique and the most delicious bread. It's not as heavy as French bread and not as light as Cuban bread.

FERDIE: For a few weeks I worked at the sandwich shop board at the Columbia Café. The board contained two notches, one for regular sandwiches, one for large. The round tips were cut off and saved for use in the kitchen. Cuban bread also came in two shapes. One was long and tubular, called sandwich bread, one flatter, thicker, and shorter, called table bread. The taste was almost the same.

The popularity of Cuban bread from Ybor City is phenomenal. La Segunda Central Bakery alone provides daily bread to supermarkets, restaurants, and homes. This bakery ships bread as far away as Alaska. One of its biggest customers is a café called Grumpy's in Little Rock, Arkansas. The bulk of the daily production goes to supermarkets and to the Columbia Restaurant.

During the height of the Columbia's popularity, the war years, the restaurant put one man in the kitchen whose sole job was cutting, heating, wrapping, and dispensing bread to the waiters. It was a full-time job, and an important one, for the presence of hot, toasty Cuban bread on the table while the customers waited for their food was one of the best things about eating at the Columbia. Many an expensive meal was ruined by the customer over-eating before the meal. Columbia Cuban bread and fresh butter is a meal in itself.

To find out how this bread is made, we went to the source, La Segunda Central Bakery, and spoke to Raymond and Tony More. After earning a Ph.D. in chemistry from Florida State University, Tony returned to his first love, baking. Along with manager George Jordan, also a Florida State alumnus and a retired fireman, we walked through the fascinating process of creating Cuban bread.

Seven ingredients make up Ybor City's Cuban bread:

1. Three types of flour: high gluten, spring wheat, and hotel and restaurant flour
2. Shortening (half beef fat and half vegetable)
3. Salt
4. Sugar (granulated)
5. Yeast
6. Water
7. Yeast food (an additive that speeds up the process)

The flour varies, depending on the weather. When it's hot, less high-gluten flour is used; when it's cold, more gluten is used.

The first step is to place the mass of ingredients in a large vat with iron rods positioned diagonally for mixing. The ingredients are mixed for ten minutes, and ice is added when needed to keep the mixture at 70° Fahrenheit. The kneading hopper is turned on and runs for forty minutes. The resultant mass looks and feels like Silly Putty.

Next to the vat-mixer is a long, flat wooden table. Its surface is lubricated with vegetable oil so that the Silly Putty mass won't stick to the table. An eight-person crew lines the table, cutting the mass into nineteen-ounce chunks with sharp scrapers. These cutters are highly experienced and can sense the exact weight of nineteen ounces. They are seldom wrong.

The crew members then knead the dough with the heel of the hand to seal the bottom. They make forty balls and place them on a flat, broad board. This board is placed in the steam box, called a proof box. When a sufficient period of time has elapsed, the rack is taken out.

The workers flatten out the lumps of dough with their forearms. This cannot be mechanized and must be done by the workers themselves. They fashion the lumps into long, tubular loaves. The forearm is placed down the middle to get the air out of the loaf and to leave an indentation down the middle.

Three green palmetto leaves are placed down the center of each loaf, one on top of the other, forming a single strand, which makes a spinelike crease on top of the loaf.

"Where do we obtain so many palmetto fronds? Well, since 1915, when we started, we've just gone out into the woods," says Tony. "But now, because the

Yankees are buying up all the property and fencing it off, we've had to start buying them. If prices keep rising, we'll have to start our own palmetto farm. Why can't other material be used to center the loaf? In our Puerto Rico bakery we use plain cord, but it is not the same. Why? I don't know.

"The palmetto leaves impart neither taste nor odor. Many bakers, failing to make the same Ybor City Cuban bread, falsely attribute their failure to the palm leaf. Nonsense."

At this point the rack of loaves is placed back in the steam box to finish "proofing" them. The loaves now measure a uniform thirty-six inches each. This measurement was arrived at by restaurateurs who wanted the loaf to make three small sandwiches or one large sandwich without loss of bread.

When the proofing is done, the racks are laid in front of huge fans, which serve to cool and dry the moisture from the loaves. The loaves are now ready for the oven. The first minute in the oven the leaf does its job: it "splits" the bread, making the crease down the center. The leaf has no other function.

The loaves are baked at 415° for thirty-five minutes. In the old days wood was used, but wood was replaced with gas or electricity when it was found that they did the job more efficiently.

At this critical point the master baker relies on expertise, rather than instruments, to determine when the bread is done. The bread must turn a golden color. It can be light, bright, or dark. All of these varieties of color are acceptable.

Tony says, "In the old days we would deliver the morning bread to each house by sticking it on a big nail on the front door frame. You could look down the street and know we had been there. Now we use UPS and air freight to deliver to the nation. The delivery cost is three times the cost of the bread. This is called progress.

"Many people buy the early-morning bread before they start their drive home and are disappointed to find that the next day the bread is hard and tasteless. The remedy for that is to wrap the fresh bread in plastic. We routinely deliver the supermarket bread in plastic.

"If one really wants to lay in a stock, the way to preserve it is to wrap it in plastic and freeze it. It will stay fresh for years. The secret is in the defrosting. The bread must be allowed to defrost slowly and naturally. It is imperative

The Columbia Café,
1945.

not to use a microwave or oven. The reason is that the moisture which is generated with defrosting must be allowed to evaporate naturally, which lets the flour base return to its normal taste. Don't take my word for it, try it."

George says, "The beauty of this process is that there is absolutely no waste. The loaves in which the palmetto leaves have slipped to the side, so that they don't have a central midline raised spine, are called monos or monkeys. These are given to supermarkets. Restaurants would reject a mono because it would

make a funny-looking Cuban sandwich. The crumbs that are left in the ovens, tables, and racks are packaged to sell for use in making croquettes, meat balls, bread pudding, et cetera."

Tony says, "One last question that always arises: Why is it that this bread is not made as deliciously outside of Tampa? Since 1915 my family has sought the answer. We have bakeries throughout the state and in Puerto Rico, but never have we been able to duplicate the Cuban bread we make in Tampa.

"Oh, we have theories, but they can't be proven. Among the most popular are, one, the water is different in Tampa; two, the palmetto leaf; three, the atmosphere in Tampa. The humidity is different.

"I'll tell you frankly, I don't know. What I do know for a fact is this: The bread in Tampa is unique. *Unico. Solo.*"

For the Columbia customers with heartier appetites there were fuller breakfasts. In the time I served breakfast at the café I had many unusual orders. Often they were unusual requests for the ingredients in omelettes, most of which were honored.

The Columbia omelettes were made either soft, with the eggs hardened on the side of the pan, then the ingredients rolled in the soft center like a jelly roll, or hard, which was a flat round omelette, solid throughout.

Some of the fillings were ham, potatoes, and onions, the most popular. Green peppers were usually mixed in with the chopped onions. Then people got strange. Cubans liked ripe plantains in the omelette; others ordered sliced chicken fillings, shrimp, crabs, lobster, sausages. One person wanted a filling of string beans and carrots. It was my first encounter with an authentic, born-again vegetarian.

I was amazed to see people put ketchup on omelettes or fried eggs. Tabasco sauce was not unusual either. The Hall of Famer was a man who ordered a half-cup of chopped garlic, two teaspoonfuls of horseradish moistened with vinegar, and two tablespoonfuls of Tabasco sauce. This fiery combination he put on a flat round omelette made with potato and peas. The order was so rare even Pijuan the master chef came out to see if the man would eat it. Eat it he did, as we watched, expecting him to burst into flames.

The other case that sticks in my mind was a drunken riveter from the hills of Tennessee who came in to eat a hearty breakfast in the hope of sobering up before reporting for work. He ordered four eggs sunny-side-up, a slab of bacon, potatoes, a large order of black Cuban coffee, and an order of toast. I served him his order, bringing an extra-long piece of buttered, toasted Cuban bread, which came wrapped in thin tissue paper. I watched in amazement as he shoveled down heaping forkfuls of eggs and bacon. He started by dipping the bread in the egg yolks, but he had not unwrapped the bread and had eaten the entire piece, wrapping and all. He got up unsteadily and paid his bill.

"Well, how was it?" I asked.

"Great, except the bread tasted papery."

"Yes, some people say that," I said, ruefully realizing I had blown the possibility of a tip.

ADELA: *Now when you start talking about eggs, there's no limit. There are fried eggs, boiled eggs, baked eggs, poached eggs, egg custard, and eggs with ham.*

Perhaps the Columbia's most spectacular egg dish is a rum omelette. An omelette filled with fruit is covered with sugar and rum and set afire. The blaze adds enough flavor to change completely the taste of the dish.

But most exotic are the Columbia's baked egg dishes such as eggs Malagueña—eggs baked in a covered casserole with green pepper, onion rings, and tomato sauce and topped with boiled shrimp and white asparagus.

Eggs and Omelettes

Huevos y Tortillas

Asparagus, Potato, and Onion Omelette

※

Tortilla de Espárragos, Papas, y Cebollas

*1 lb. fresh asparagus, steamed and
 cut in 2-inch pieces*
*2 medium-size potatoes, peeled and
 sliced in half-moons, ⅛ inch thick*
6 large eggs

*1 large Spanish onion, thinly sliced
 in half-moons*
2 garlic cloves, mashed
⅓ cup extra-virgin olive oil
Salt and pepper to taste

Heat oil in 9-inch omelette pan. Fry garlic until golden and discard. Add potato slices; cook over medium heat. Add onions after 5 minutes. Lift and turn potatoes and onions as they cook. When potatoes are tender, add asparagus and mix thoroughly.

In a large bowl, beat eggs, salt, and pepper with a fork or wire whisk until slightly foamy. Add potatoes, onions, and asparagus to eggs; drain vegetables with a slotted spoon as you add them. Return eggs and vegetable mixture to same skillet, adding more oil if necessary, so that eggs will not stick. Spread evenly and cook over medium heat, shaking pan.

When eggs leave sides of pan, invert a plate over the pan and flip omelette onto plate. Slide omelette back into pan to brown on other side. Repeat this process one more time. Serve hot or at room temperature on a round china or glass platter. Serves 4.

Cauliflower Omelette

❦

Tortilla de Coliflor

1 head cauliflower, separated into
   florets
1 large onion, thinly sliced in
   half-moons
3 garlic cloves, mashed

⅓ cup extra-virgin olive oil
6 eggs
Salt and pepper to taste
1 tablespoon lemon juice

Boil cauliflower in salted water with lemon juice. Remove cauliflower when barely tender; drain. Fry garlic in oil until golden and discard. Sauté onion for 5 minutes in same oil. Add cauliflower and cook over low heat for 5 minutes. Beat eggs, salt, and pepper in a large bowl until frothy. Add cauliflower and onion, using a slotted spoon to drain oil before adding. Mix well with egg and return to pan, adding more oil if necessary. Spread evenly and cook over medium heat.

When eggs leave sides of pan, invert a plate over the pan and flip omelette onto plate. Slide omelette back into pan to brown on other side. Repeat this process one more time. Serve hot. Serves 4.

Eggs Malagueña

❧

Huevos Malagueña

8 eggs

2 tablespoons extra-virgin olive
   oil

6 fresh or canned plum tomatoes,
   peeled, seeded, chopped

2 garlic cloves, minced

1 medium onion, finely chopped

1 green pepper, finely chopped

¼ lb. shrimps, peeled, deveined,
   and cooked

4 white asparagus tips

¼ lb. smoked ham, cut in cubes

1 **chorizo** (Spanish sausage), sliced

⅓ cup green peas, cooked

¼ teaspoon paprika

Salt to taste

Heat olive oil in skillet. Sauté garlic and onion until onion is limp. Add tomatoes, paprika, salt, and green pepper. Cover and cook over low heat for 10 minutes.

Sauté ham and *chorizo* in another skillet for 5 minutes. Add shrimp and heat. Pour tomato mixture in equal parts into 4 individual ramekins, re-serving small amount for topping. Break two eggs in each dish. Add ham, *chorizo*, and shrimp in equal parts; top each dish with a little more tomato mixture. Bake at 400° until eggs are set, about 6 minutes. Garnish with peas and asparagus tips. Serves 4.

Eggs with Vegetables, Shrimp, and Ham

Pisto Manchego

12 eggs

½ lb. pork loin, cut in small chunks

1 lb. shrimps, peeled, deveined,
  and cooked

¼ lb. smoked ham, chopped

2 potatoes, peeled, diced, and fried

3 roasted red peppers, chopped

3 onions, chopped

2 green peppers, chopped

4 tablespoons extra-virgin olive oil

4 garlic cloves, minced

1 tablespoon salt

¼ teaspoon pepper

1 10-oz. package frozen tender tiny
  green peas, cooked

2 tablespoons dry sherry

6 small tomatoes, peeled, seeded,
  and chopped

¼ cup peanut oil

½ cup water

Brown pork loin chunks in peanut oil; add ½ cup water. Cook over low heat until tender. Drain. Sauté onions, green peppers, and garlic in olive oil until onions are transparent. Add tomatoes and sauté until liquid has evaporated. Add red peppers, shrimp, pork, ham, peas, and potatoes. Stir and add sherry. Beat eggs with salt and pepper until blended, add to contents in skillet, and scramble until eggs are cooked. Serves 6–8.

Potato and Onion Omelette

Tortilla de Papas y Cebollas

½ cup extra-virgin olive oil

2 garlic cloves, mashed

4 large potatoes, peeled and cut in
  ⅛-inch half-moons

1 large Spanish onion, thinly sliced
  in half-moons

6 large eggs

Salt and pepper to taste

Heat oil in 9-inch omelette pan. Fry garlic until golden and discard. Add potato slices and cook over medium heat. Add onions after 5 minutes; cook until potatoes are tender. Lift and turn potatoes and onions as they cook.

In a large bowl beat eggs with a fork or wire whisk until slightly foamy; add salt and pepper to taste. Add potatoes and onions to eggs, draining with a slotted spoon before you add them. Return egg and potato mixture to same skillet, adding more oil if necessary so that eggs will not stick. Spread evenly and cook over medium heat, shaking pan.

When eggs leave sides of pan, invert a plate over the pan and flip omelette onto plate. Slide omelette back into pan to brown on other side. Repeat this process one more time. Serve hot or at room temperature on a round china or glass platter. Serves 4.

Ripe Plantain Omelette

Tortilla de Plátanos

2 ripe plantains
4 eggs

Peanut oil (about ½ cup)
Salt to taste

Peel plantains and slice diagonally about ¼ inch thick.

Heat oil in 8-inch skillet. Fry plantain slices until golden. Drain. Beat eggs in a bowl until frothy. Add plantains and salt. In same skillet, leaving enough oil to prevent eggs from sticking, return eggs and plantains. Cook over medium heat, spreading evenly. Invert omelette and slide back into skillet to brown on other side. Repeat this process one more time. Serve hot. Serves 2.

Rum Omelette

Tortilla al Ron

8 eggs
1 cup stewed apples (drained), or
   1 cup pineapple tidbits (drained),
   or 1 cup guava (drained and
   chopped guava shells), or
   1 cup fruit cocktail (drained)

4 tablespoons sugar
¼ teaspoon salt
2 tablespoons sherry
3 tablespoons butter
⅓ cup white rum, heated

Combine eggs, salt, and half of sugar. Beat until light. Add drained fruit and sherry to eggs.

Melt butter in a nonstick omelette pan. Add egg mixture and cook over medium heat. Make sure that eggs do not brown. When eggs are set, fold omelette in half, giving it a half-moon shape. Cook briefly and flip over; cook until eggs are done. Transfer omelette to a flameproof platter. Sprinkle remaining 2 tablespoons of sugar on top and pour heated rum around omelette. Set aflame. Spoon flaming rum over omelette. Serve immediately. Serves 6.

Shrimp Omelette

Tortilla de Camarones

4 eggs
18 medium-size shrimps, peeled,
   deveined, and sliced in half
   lengthwise

1 medium-size onion, chopped
2 garlic cloves, mashed
¼ cup extra-virgin olive oil
Salt and pepper to taste

Heat oil in 8-inch skillet or omelette pan. Fry garlic until golden and discard. Add onion and sauté until transparent. Add shrimp and sauté until they turn pink. Beat eggs with salt and pepper in a large bowl until frothy. Add shrimp mixture and stir well. Return to pan, adding more oil if needed. Cook over medium heat until eggs are set. Invert a plate over the pan, flip omelette onto plate, and return to pan to brown on other side. Repeat process one more time. Serve hot. Serves 2.

Spanish Omelette

Tortilla à la Española

¼ cup chopped ham	2 teaspoons green peas (cooked)
¼ cup diced potatoes	4 eggs
¼ cup sliced mushrooms	¼ cup olive oil
2 tablespoons chopped pimentos or	Salt and pepper to taste
roasted red peppers	Vegetable oil for frying potatoes

Deep-fry potatoes in vegetable oil. Drain. Beat eggs until frothy, add potatoes and rest of ingredients except olive oil, and combine well.

Heat olive oil in 6-inch omelette pan. Add egg mixture, shaking pan and stirring. When eggs leave sides of pan, invert omelette onto a plate. Return to pan and brown lightly on other side. May be served hot or at room temperature. Serves 2.

Chapter Three

CASIMIRO I:
THE ROMANCE BEGINS

FERDIE: Casimiro Hernandez I, born in Matanzas, Cuba, was married with two children when he was impressed into the Spanish navy. At Havana he jumped ship and fled into the city. By 1904 he had enough money to take his family to the thriving little town of Tampa on Florida's west coast. There, amidst the scrub palmettos and rattlesnakes, an immigrant community was taking shape. Cubans, Spaniards, and Italians were working in the expanding cigar industry, and Ybor City was being born.

By 1905, Casimiro had saved enough money to start a small café on the outer edge of town. On the corner of Seventh Avenue and Twenty-second, the main street, he opened the Columbia Café. Casimiro was an intensely loyal patriot. He felt a deep love for the country that had taken him in and accepted his family and that was now his home. This loyalty and love for America, also called Columbia, the Gem of the Ocean, led him to name his little café the "Columbia," under which he added, "The Gem of All Spanish Restaurants." It was a presumptuous name for such a small, insignificant structure, but it turned out to be prophetic.

The outskirts of town had the feel of an old-time Wild West town. Once a man rode his horse through the swinging doors of the café and, without dismounting, ordered a beer. Without blinking an eye, Casimiro drew an eighteen-ounce draft beer and smiled. The standard of pleasing the public was set and never varied. At the Columbia Restaurant customers expected and got first-rate service with continental professionalism.

The Columbia Restaurant soon became known for three main dishes: Casimiro's unique garbanzo soup, the original Cuban sandwich, and *arroz con pollo,* a chicken and yellow rice dish that was filling and delicious.

Casimiro Hernandez I, founder, 1926.

ADELA: *My grandfather was an intrepid and innovative person. Being of Spanish ancestry, he was very knowledgeable about Spanish cuisine, and he simplified such classics as* **cocido madrileño,** *a boiled Spanish equivalent of French pot-au-feu.* **Cocido** *was traditionally served in two steps, first the broth, then the main course of meats, garbanzos, and potatoes. He came up with the idea that all should be served together. That's what became Spanish bean soup. It's from Tampa. You cannot order Spanish bean soup in Spain. They don't know what it is. But here it became a mainstay of all Spanish-Cuban restaurants, first in Florida and eventually throughout the United States.*

The authentic Cuban sandwich has roast pork that has been marinated Cuban-style with sour orange juice, garlic, and oregano. Sugar-cured ham cut in thin slices is a very important part of this delicious sandwich. And it has to have hard salami, not bologna which some people use. There's also Swiss cheese and sour pickle. Most everyone today uses dill pickle, but it should be sour pickle. Yellow mustard is spread on one of the slices. It has to be cut diagonally, and it has

Exterior of café. The porthole was for takeout orders.

to be wrapped in tissue paper. If it's not wrapped, with a toothpick through the paper, it's not right.

Arroz con pollo *is a simple, classic Spanish combination of chicken sautéed in olive oil and cooked along with rice, onions, peppers, saffron, and other herbs. (See pages 48, 105, and 184 for recipes.)*

FERDIE: Soon the Columbia Café was doing so well that Casimiro decided to expand. Next door was a restaurant called La Fonda, which was failing. Calling in the owner, Manuel Garcia, Casimiro proposed a merger. They put a door between the café and La Fonda and united the two businesses. The first flu epidemic of 1918 had come and gone, and the money started to flow.

By this time business was booming, but the profligate spending of the generous Casimiro always had the restaurant teetering on the brink of financial disaster. He was still charging impoverished cigar makers five dollars a *month* for daily meals, which was, all things considered, a losing proposition. Luckily the cuisine was so superior and the service so expert that the townspeople of Tampa, as well as the burgeoning tourist trade, were keeping the restaurant afloat.

Casimiro died on March 11, 1929, and his oldest son, Casimiro II, Adela's father, became the restaurant's owner.

ADELA: *If my grandfather had not died when I was eight years old, I'd probably have grown up to be spoiled rotten. How I loved him! I was the apple of his eye. He indulged me shamelessly, and I called him **Viejo** (old man), in the most affectionate way.*

One Christmas I had my eye on a fancy dollhouse. Every chance I got I'd go to the toy store on Seventh and look longingly at the desired dollhouse, but my mother reminded me that the fifty dollars it cost was too dear for their budget. It was a ridiculous price in those days when a cigar maker was making six dollars a week.

Hearing about it, Viejo came to my house and gave my mom a fifty-dollar bill and told her to let Santa Claus bring his adored Adelita the dollhouse.

Well, my mom was a warmhearted person, but she was also very practical. She told me that I needed a winter coat more than a dollhouse. Oh, my heart was broken. I thought I would not live through Christmas.

The first chance I got, I crept onto Viejo's knee, looking forlorn, my eyes wa-

In La Fonda, 1920 (standing, l. to r.): Nicanor, El Rey, Manuel Garcia, and Casimiro II.

La Fonda, filled to capacity for lunch, 1942.

tering. I spilled out my tale of woe, with very little prompting. Viejo heard me out, got a stern look on his face, and headed for the kitchen.

I was not surprised to find a dollhouse under my tree. Viejo did not usually interfere with my mother, but fifty dollars was nothing to him. Perhaps it's a lesson for us. Money, in and of itself, is worthless. Better to make a child happy was his way. Mine, too, I think.

At the age of eight, already proficient at the piano, I was patiently learning "The Merry Widow Waltz" for my grandfather. One morning I was summoned by my cousin from school. I don't know why, but in that moment, I felt something had happened to my beloved Viejo. I was shattered by the news that he had died of an overwhelming heart attack at the age of fifty-nine. He died calling for me.

Looking back now, I appreciate the value of a treasured grandparent. They love without a qualification. They don't need to worry about discipline. They give pure, undiluted love.

From Viejo I got the love of music, art, and culture. He encouraged and inspired me to play the piano and to excel. To this day I cannot hear "The Merry Widow Waltz" without crying freely.

SOUPS

✿

SOPAS

Asturian Navy Bean Soup

※

Fabada Asturiana

1 lb. white kidney beans, dried,
   or 2 16-oz. cans great northern
   beans
½ lb. salt pork, cut in bite-size
   pieces
1 smoked ham hock (about 1 lb.)
2 cloves garlic, crushed

1 **morcilla** (Spanish blood sausage)
1 **chorizo** (Spanish sausage),
   cut into ¼-inch rounds
2 tablespoons extra-virgin olive oil
2 potatoes, peeled and cut in
   eighths
Salt to taste

The night before, soak beans in enough water to cover; skip this step if using canned beans. In the same water in which they have been soaked, place beans in soup pot; for canned beans, use liquid in can. Add blood sausage, ham hock, and salt pork. Bring to a boil and add ½ cup cold water. Cover and simmer slowly for about 2 hours, adding water if necessary.

Heat oil in skillet, brown garlic lightly, and add *chorizo*. Add to beans and then add potatoes and salt. Cook over low heat until potatoes are tender. Let sit for 1 to 2 hours before serving. Reheat. Serves 6.

Beef Broth

Caldo de Res

1 flank steak (about 1½ lbs.)
2½ quarts water
2 large onions, quartered
1 green pepper, cut in strips
6 garlic cloves, crushed

2 tomatoes, peeled, seeded,
    and cut in quarters
1 bay leaf
1 carrot
Salt to taste

Cut flank steak into 4 x 4-inch pieces. Place in stock pot and cover with water. Boil; skim foam off surface. Add rest of ingredients, cover, and boil until beef is tender. Strain, saving vegetables for brown sauce or shredded beef (see pp. 201, 112). Makes about 1 quart.

Black Bean Soup

Frijoles Negros

1 lb. black beans, dried
2 quarts water
2 medium onions, chopped fine
1 bay leaf
2 green peppers, cut in strips
½ cup olive oil
1 teaspoon oregano

4 cloves garlic, minced
¼ teaspoon ground cumin
1 tablespoon salt
½ teaspoon black pepper
White rice, cooked
Chopped onions for garnish

Before washing beans, spread on flat surface and pick out broken beans and foreign particles. Wash beans thoroughly and soak overnight in 2 quarts of water.

Next day, pour beans and water into a 4-quart soup kettle; bring to a boil. Cover and cook over medium heat.

Meanwhile, in a skillet, sauté onions and green peppers in olive oil until light golden. Add crushed oregano, bay leaf, cumin, and garlic. Add mixture to beans, stirring well. Add salt and pepper and cook slowly over low heat, covered, until beans are tender (at least 1 hour). Serve over white rice and top with chopped onions. Serves 4.

Chicken Broth

❧

Caldo de Pollo

1 3½- to 4-lb. chicken and giblets
   (not liver)
4 medium-size onions, peeled
   and cut in quarters
1 carrot, scraped and cut in pieces
6 garlic cloves, mashed

1 2-inch strip green pepper
5 quarts water
Salt to taste
¼ teaspoon saffron or yellow
   food coloring

Place chicken and giblets (whole or cut up) in a large stock pot. Add water and bring to a boil; remove foam. Add rest of ingredients. Cover and boil 1½ hours. Remove from stove and strain. Refrigerate clear broth until fat rises and gels solidify. Skim fat from top. Chicken may be cut up and added to the soup or used for making a filling for *empanadillas* (turnovers) or croquettes. Makes about 2½ quarts.

Collard Greens Soup

※

Berzada

1 lb. great northern beans, dried

½ lb. smoked ham, cut in small pieces (ham bone, if available, is great for flavor)

2 potatoes, peeled and cut in eighths

1 bunch collard greens, washed, tough stems removed, cut into ½-inch strips

½ lb. salt pork, cut in 1-inch pieces

1 onion, chopped

4 garlic cloves, minced

1 **morcilla** (Spanish blood sausage), thinly sliced

2 **chorizos** (Spanish sausages), thinly sliced

¼ cup extra-virgin olive oil

1 quart water

Salt to taste

Soak beans overnight. Drain. In a large pot, cover beans with 1 quart fresh water. Add ham and ham bone. When beans are partially cooked, add greens. Cook until beans and greens are tender, adding water if necessary.

In frying pan, heat olive oil. Add salt pork. When fat is rendered, add onion and garlic. Sauté until limp. Add to cooked beans along with potatoes, *morcilla*, and *chorizo*. Season with salt, if needed. This soup is better after it sits for 2 or 3 hours. Reheat and serve very hot. Serves 6.

Corn Chowder Cuban Style

Guiso de Maíz

1 large onion, chopped
1 large green pepper, cut in strips
4 cloves garlic, minced
Half of an 8-oz. can of tomato
   sauce
2 bay leaves
1 lb. pork loin, cut in 2-inch cubes
½ lb. smoked ham, cut in small
   pieces
½ cup peanut oil

2 medium-size potatoes, peeled
   and cut in 8 pieces
1 butternut squash, peeled and
   cut in 3-inch squares
2 cups chicken broth
2 15-oz. cans whole kernel corn
1 15-oz. can cream-style corn
2 ears fresh corn, cut into 2-inch
   pieces
Salt and pepper to taste

Heat oil in a heavy-bottomed 6-quart pot. Brown pork cubes. Add chopped onion, green pepper, garlic, bay leaves, and tomato sauce. Cover and simmer until pork is tender. Add broth, potatoes, squash, and ham. When potatoes and squash are tender, add canned corn and fresh corn. Cook for 5 minutes, stirring frequently so corn will not stick to bottom of pan. Salt and pepper to taste. This chowder can be made hours before serving. Serves 6.

Crazy Soup

❧

Sopa Loca

1 flank steak (1 to 1½ lbs.), cut in 1-inch squares
3 quarts water
1 large onion, chopped
1 medium-size green pepper, cut in strips
6 cloves garlic, chopped
2 tomatoes, peeled, seeded, and cut in chunks
1 bay leaf

2 sweet potatoes, peeled and cut in 1-inch cubes
4 chunks frozen yucca
2 medium-size white potatoes, peeled and cut in chunks
1 small butternut squash, cut in 2-inch chunks
Salt and pepper to taste
2 medium-ripe plantains, peeled and cut in 2-inch rounds
2 ears corn, cut in 2-inch rounds

Boil flank steak in water, removing foam. Lower heat and add onion, green pepper, garlic, tomatoes, and bay leaf. Cover and boil slowly until meat is tender (approximately 1½ hours). Strain; discard vegetables and herbs. Set meat aside. Add sweet potatoes, yucca, white potatoes, squash, salt, and pepper to broth and cook over medium heat. When these vegetables are almost tender, add plantains, corn, and flank steak; cook until corn and plantains are done. Serve very hot. Serves 4.

Cuban Creole Stew

❧

Ajiaco

¼ lb. **tasajo** *(dried beef, available in Latin American stores), cut in small pieces*

½ lb. *flank steak, cut in 2-inch squares*

½ lb. *pork (for stewing), cut in 2-inch squares*

1 lb. *malanga (taro), available frozen in Latin American stores*

1 lb. *yucca, cut in 2-inch chunks*

½ lb. *sweet potatoes, peeled and cut in 8 rounds*

1 lb. *butternut squash, cut in 2-inch chunks*

Juice of 1 lemon

2 *ears of corn, cut in 2-inch rounds*

1 *green plantain, peeled and cut in 2-inch rounds*

1 *medium-ripe plantain, peeled and cut in 2-inch rounds*

1 *large onion, chopped*

1 *green pepper, cut in strips*

3 *garlic cloves, minced*

1 *8-oz. can tomato sauce*

2 *tablespoons peanut oil*

Salt and pepper to taste

3 *quarts water*

Soak *tasajo* overnight; discard water. In a large pot, place *tasajo,* flank steak, pork, and 3 quarts water. Cover and bring to a boil. Remove foam, cover, and boil for 1 hour.

Heat oil in skillet. Sauté onion and green pepper until limp. Add garlic and tomato sauce. Add mixture to meat broth and stir. Add rest of ingredients in the following order: malanga, yucca, sweet potatoes, squash, green plantain, lemon juice, corn, medium-ripe plantain, salt, and pepper. Boil until all are tender. Serve hot in soup bowls. Serves 6.

Fresh Grated Corn Mush

Tamal en Cazuela

1½ lbs. pork, cut in cubes	2 green peppers, chopped
1 tablespoon garlic powder	2 teaspoons garlic, finely minced
¼ cup lemon juice	2 cups tomato sauce
¼ cup orange juice	2 bay leaves
1 tablespoon salt	5 cups fresh or frozen corn, grated
½ teaspoon black pepper	(available already grated and
¾ cup peanut oil	frozen in Latin American stores)
4 onions, chopped	7 cups water

Marinate pork in garlic powder, lemon and orange juice, salt, and pepper for at least two hours. Heat ¼ cup oil in frying pan. Brown pork cubes, remove from pan, and drain. Set aside. In a large saucepan, sauté onions, green peppers, and minced garlic in ½ cup oil until limp. Add tomato sauce, bay leaves, and pork. Cover and cook until pork is tender; add some of the water if needed. When pork is tender, add corn and rest of water. Stir and cook for 45 minutes over low heat, stirring often so corn will not stick to bottom of pan. Serves 8.

Garlic Soup

Sopa de Ajo

6 tablespoons extra-virgin olive oil	1½ quarts chicken broth
8 garlic cloves, thoroughly mashed	1 tablespoon paprika
6 thin slices Cuban or French	4 eggs
bread	Salt to taste

Fry garlic in olive oil, using an ovenproof casserole (tureen type). When garlic is golden, remove and reserve. In same oil, fry bread slices slowly until golden on both sides. Reserve. Add broth, paprika, and salt to casserole; bring to a boil. Add garlic to broth. Add bread slices. Beat eggs in a separate bowl and add to broth, stirring; cook briefly. Serve very hot. Serves 4.

Indian Seafood Soup

Sopa India

¾ cup scallops

1 large onion, finely chopped

¾ cup oysters, shucked

2 garlic cloves, minced

¾ cup shrimp, peeled and deveined

4 stone crab or blue crab claws,
    steamed and cracked

1 10-oz. package frozen sliced okra

2 cans Campbell's green pea soup

1 10-oz. package frozen whole
    kernel corn

⅛ cup olive oil

2 tablespoons sherry

Salt and pepper to taste

Make green pea soup according to directions; puree in food processor. In soup pot, sauté onion in olive oil until limp. Add garlic, being careful not to burn. Add seafood, except crabs, and sauté for two minutes. Add corn, okra, and pea soup puree. Simmer for two additional minutes; add crab claws just before serving. Add sherry. Season with salt and pepper. Serves 4.

Lentil Soup

❧

Sopa de Lentejas

1 lb. lentils, dried
3 quarts water
1 medium onion, cut in quarters
1 medium green pepper, cut in
    quarters
1 ham hock (about ½ lb.)
¼ cup extra-virgin olive oil

2 onions, chopped
4 garlic cloves, finely minced
1 bay leaf
1 carrot, scraped and cut into thin
    rounds
2 medium-size potatoes, peeled
    and cut in small cubes

Wash lentils well, picking out any foreign particles. In a large pot, soak lentils in 3 quarts water for one to two hours. Add ham hock and quartered onion and green pepper; boil gently for about 45 minutes. Meanwhile, heat oil in a skillet and sauté chopped onion until wilted. Add garlic, bay leaf, and carrot. Add to lentils and bring to a boil. When lentils are tender, add potatoes and cook until fork-tender. Remove meat from ham hock, and add meat to soup. Serve hot. Serves 4.

Navy Bean Soup Cuban Style

※

Potaje de Judías à la Criolla

1 cup navy beans, dried, or 3
    15-oz. cans great northern beans
2½ quarts water
2 bay leaves
¼ cup extra-virgin olive oil
4 cloves garlic, finely chopped
1 teaspoon oregano
1 2-oz. piece salt pork (rind
    removed), cut in small pieces

1 large onion, finely chopped
1 green pepper, cut in strips
1 8-oz. can tomato sauce
1 medium-size potato, peeled and
    cut in chunks
1 butternut squash (seeds removed),
    cut in chunks
½ lb. boneless smoked ham, diced
Salt and pepper to taste

Rinse dried navy beans in cold water, pick over to remove foreign particles, and soak covered in water overnight. Drain beans and place them in a large saucepan with 2½ quarts water, bay leaves, and salt pork. Bring to a boil, reduce heat, and simmer, covered, until tender, 1 to 1½ hours, adding water if necessary. (If using canned beans, the above step is unnecessary, since beans are already cooked.)

In a medium-size skillet, heat olive oil and sauté onion, green pepper, garlic, oregano, ham, and tomato sauce for 10 minutes. In a separate saucepan, boil squash chunks for 5 minutes. Remove from water, adding same water to tomato mixture. Peel squash. When beans are tender, add tomato mixture, potato, salt, pepper, and squash. Continue cooking another 30 minutes. Remove salt pork and discard. Serve in soup bowls. Serves 6.

Okra Stew Cuban Style

Quimbombó à la Criolla

3 lbs. fresh okra

1½ lbs. pork cubes, cut for stew

½ lb. smoked ham, cut in 1-inch
   cubes

¼ cup extra-virgin olive oil

1 large Spanish onion, chopped

1 8-oz. can tomato sauce

1 green pepper, cut in 1-inch strips

4 garlic cloves, finely chopped

2 cups chicken broth

2 medium-ripe plantains

1 bay leaf

Salt and pepper to taste

Wash okra and pat dry. Cut into ½-inch rounds, removing stems. Set aside. In a large saucepan or casserole, heat olive oil and sauté onion, green pepper, and garlic. Add pork and brown for 10 minutes. Add bay leaf and tomato sauce and cook over low heat until pork is tender; add some of the chicken broth if sauce gets dry. Add ham and chicken broth. Bring to a boil, add okra, and cook for 10 minutes. Season with salt and pepper. Drop plantain dumplings into stew and simmer 5 minutes. Serves 4.

PLANTAIN DUMPLINGS

Cut plantains into 2-inch rounds. Boil until tender, leaving skin on. Drain and peel. Mash thoroughly and make dumplings about the size of a golf ball.

Peas and Potato Soup

Potaje de Chícharos

3 15-oz. cans tiny green peas
   (preferably LeSueur)
¼ cup extra-virgin olive oil
1 large onion, chopped
2 garlic cloves, finely minced

2 **chorizos** *(Spanish sausages),
   cut in ¼-inch rounds*
2 medium-size potatoes, peeled
   and diced
1 bay leaf

Heat oil in saucepan, sauté onion lightly, and add garlic. Add *chorizos,* peas (liquid and all), and bay leaf. When mixture boils, add potatoes and cook over low heat until potatoes are tender. Serves 4.

Potato, Onion, and Cabbage Soup

Sopa de Papas, Cebollas, y Col

2 large potatoes, peeled and cut in
   ¼-inch half-moon slices
5 cups chicken broth
2 large onions, thinly sliced in
   half-moons

1 tablespoon butter
¼ cup olive oil
3 cups coarsely shredded cabbage
3 whole garlic cloves

In soup pot, melt butter at medium heat (do not brown). Add olive oil. Brown garlic lightly and discard. Brown potatoes lightly and add onions and cabbage. Heat chicken broth separately. When onions and cabbage are limp, add hot chicken broth to soup pot and boil slowly until vegetables are tender. Serves 4.

Puree of Black Beans with Sherry

Puré de Frijoles Negros con Vino de Jerez

*2 quarts cooked black beans
    (see p. 34)
Chicken broth*

*½ cup dry sherry
Garlic bread croutons*

Puree beans in blender or food processor. Transfer to a deep saucepan. Add enough chicken broth to give soup the consistency of a cream soup. Bring to a boil, remove from heat, and add sherry. Serve in deep soup bowls, topped with a few croutons. Serves 4.

Puree of Spanish Bean Soup

Puré de Potaje de Garbanzos

*2 quarts Spanish bean soup
    (see p. 48)
Chicken broth*

*2 hard-boiled eggs, chopped
Chopped parsley*

Puree soup in a blender or food processor. Transfer to a deep saucepan. Add enough chicken broth to give soup the consistency of a cream soup. Serve in soup bowls, topping with chopped egg and parsley. Serves 4.

Quarter-Hour Soup

❧

Sopa al Cuarto de Hora

Step 1

1 grouper head (or any other whitefish)

4 bay leaves

4 garlic cloves, mashed

2 onions, cut in chunks

3 ripe tomatoes, peeled, seeded, and cut in chunks

2 carrots, cut in chunks

4 quarts water

1 celery stalk, cut in chunks

Dash of saffron or yellow food coloring

Salt and pepper to taste

In a large pot, boil all ingredients, skimming off scum as it surfaces. Reduce heat and cook down to 2 quarts (about 1½ hours). Strain and set broth aside.

Step 2

10 ounces grouper fillets, cut in medium-size pieces

1 medium-size onion, finely chopped

10 ounces shrimp, peeled and deveined

4 garlic cloves, finely minced

10 ounces scallops

¾ cup tomato sauce

12 mussels, shelled

12 clams, shelled

1 teaspoon Pernod

1 lb. lobster, shelled, cut in medium pieces

½ cup extra-virgin olive oil

¼ cup lemon juice

½ teaspoon saffron

Salt and pepper to taste

¼ cup brandy

In heavy saucepan, sauté onion and garlic in olive oil until onion is transparent. Add seafood and sauté briefly. Add brandy and flambé. Add tomato sauce, heated seafood broth (from step 1), saffron, Pernod, salt, and pepper; cook for 5 minutes. Add lemon juice just before serving. Serves 4.

Note: Other kinds of seafood may be substituted.

Spanish Bean Soup

Potaje de Garbanzos

½ lb. garbanzo beans, dried
  (chickpeas)
1 ham bone
1 beef bone
2 quarts water
1 tablespoon salt
¼ lb. salt pork, cut in thin strips

1 onion, finely chopped
1 **chorizo** (Spanish sausage),
  sliced in thin rounds
2 potatoes, peeled and cut in
  quarters
Pinch of saffron
½ teaspoon paprika

Wash garbanzos. Soak overnight with 1 tablespoon salt in enough water to cover beans. Drain the salted water from the beans. Place beans in 4-quart soup kettle; add 2 quarts of water and ham and beef bones. Cook for 45 minutes over low heat, skimming foam from the top. Fry salt pork slowly in a skillet. Add chopped onion and sauté lightly. Add to beans along with potatoes, paprika, and saffron. Add salt to taste. When potatoes are tender, remove from heat and add *chorizo*. Serve hot in deep soup bowls. Serves 4.

Spanish Cold Tomato Soup

❧

Gazpacho Andaluz

2 cups water

1 medium onion, finely chopped

3 ripe tomatoes, peeled, seeded,
  and chopped

1 cucumber, peeled and sliced

4 tablespoons white vinegar

2 teaspoons salt

3 cloves garlic, crushed

4 slices bread, cut in pieces

4 tablespoons olive oil

GARNISH

1 cucumber, diced

1 green pepper, diced

1 medium onion, finely chopped

1 tomato, finely chopped

1 cup croutons

Combine first nine ingredients and let stand for 1 hour. Puree in a blender and chill in refrigerator. Garnish and serve chilled in soup bowls. Serves 4.

Note: Gazpacho is an old dish that comes from Roman and Greek literature, where it is described as a "drinkable food." The word **gazpacho** *comes from an Arabic word meaning "soaked bread."*

Turnip Greens Soup

※

Caldo Gallego

1 lb. great northern beans, dried
1 lb. ham hock
¼ lb. salt pork, cut in pieces
½ lb. beef chuck, cut in 2-inch pieces
1 beef bone
1 onion, chopped
*1 **chorizo** (Spanish sausage),*
  sliced in thin rounds

2 quarts water
3 medium potatoes, peeled and
  quartered
2 turnips, peeled and quartered
2 cups turnip greens, coarsely
  chopped, thick stems removed
Salt to taste

Soak beans overnight in water in a large pot. Next day, add salt pork, ham hock, beef bone, beef chuck, and onion. In same water, bring beans to a boil and skim off foam. Cover and simmer over low heat for about 2 hours, or until beans are almost tender. Add potatoes, turnips, and greens. Cook about 30 minutes or until potatoes are tender. Add *chorizo*. Let stand for 2 to 3 hours before serving. Heat and serve in large soup bowls. Serves 4.

Salads
✺
Ensaladas

Pumpkin, String Beans, Egg, and Onion Salad

—————————————— ❧ ——————————————

Ensalada de Calabaza, Judías Verdes, y Cebolla

1 lb. tender string beans
½ lb. Cuban pumpkin or butternut
  squash or white potatoes
1 large Spanish onion, thinly sliced
2 cloves garlic, mashed

Salt and pepper to taste
4 hard-boiled eggs, cut in half
½ cup olive oil
¼ cup white wine vinegar

Wash and remove ends of string beans. Boil water (enough to cover beans) in a large pot with garlic and salt. Plunge string beans in water and cover. When water returns to a boil, uncover pot and cook beans over medium heat for 5 minutes. Drain. Boil pumpkin or squash or potatoes in enough water to cover, leaving skin on. When fork-tender, remove from water, drain, and cool. Peel and cut in bite-size chunks.

Arrange string beans, pumpkin, hard-boiled eggs (cut in half), and onion slices on a platter. Mix vinegar and olive oil, pour over salad, and add salt and pepper to taste. Serves 4.

San Isidro Salad

❧

Ensalada de San Isidro

1 head Boston or Bibb lettuce,
   torn into bite-size pieces
2 large tomatoes, cut in eighths
4 thin slices Spanish onion
1 7-oz. can chunk white tuna,
   drained and separated

¼ cup extra-virgin olive oil
¼ cup white wine vinegar
½ teaspoon garlic powder
Salt and pepper to taste

In small mixing bowl, combine oil, vinegar, garlic powder, salt, and pepper to make dressing. In salad bowl, carefully mix lettuce, tomato, onion, and tuna. Add dressing and toss lightly. Serves 2 as main dish.

1905 Salad

❧

Ensalada 1905

½ head iceberg lettuce

2 ripe tomatoes, cut in eighths

2 stalks celery, sliced

½ cup Swiss cheese, cut in julienne
   strips

½ cup ham, cut in julienne strips
   (or turkey or shrimp)

¼ cup green Spanish olives, pitted

2 teaspoons grated Romano
   cheese

Toss together all salad ingredients except Romano cheese.

DRESSING

⅛ cup white wine vinegar

½ cup extra-virgin Spanish
   olive oil

4 cloves garlic, minced

1 teaspoon Worcestershire sauce

Salt and pepper to taste

1 teaspoon oregano

2 teaspoons lemon juice

Mix garlic, oregano, and Worcestershire sauce in a bowl. Beat until smooth with a wire whisk. Add olive oil, gradually beating to form an emulsion. Stir in vinegar and lemon juice and season with salt and pepper. Add dressing to salad and toss well. Add Romano cheese and toss one more time. Serves 4.

Chapter Four

CASIMIRO II:
THE GOLDEN YEARS

FERDIE: Part of what Casimiro II inherited was a mountain of debt, an apparently insurmountable sum, and an unstable economy. The beginnings of the Great Depression caused the restaurant's business to take a nosedive. At one point Casimiro considered closing the restaurant, but he had faith in the business, a stout heart, and a dream of a bigger and better Columbia.

By 1935 Casimiro had thought up the idea of building an elegant dining room with music and dancing, the likes of which had never been seen in the southern part of the United States. His dream far exceeded his pocketbook, but he was not his father's son for nothing. Backed by the strong support of his wife, Carmita, and his belief in his plan, Casimiro put on his best suit and went in to see Mr. Simpson of the Columbia Bank.

ADELA: *My daddy told Mr. Simpson about his dream of an elegant, one-of-a-kind room. The sympathetic Mr. Simpson knew all about the Columbia's roller-coaster finances and about Viejo, who spent money wildly when he had it.*

"How much do you need?" he asked.

"Thirty-five thousand dollars will do it," my daddy said, looking Mr. Simpson in the eye.

"If that is what it takes, you have it, Casimiro." And with a handshake my daddy had the money to see his dream come true.

I remember it vividly because the next day I was in the bathroom that served our two adjacent bedrooms, getting dressed to go to school. My daddy came into

56

my parents' bedroom, and I heard him tell my mother that Mr. Simpson had given him the thirty-five thousand dollars on a handshake. He sounded very worried. Then I heard him say, "Carmita, if this room is not a successful venture, I'll have to blow my brains out."

Well, I thought I'd faint right there. I'd never heard my daddy talk like that. He was a serious man, not given to idle talk, boasts, or threats. He usually said exactly what he meant. Then I heard my mother say, "Casimiro, this room is going to work. Never say a thing like that to me again!"

Casimiro II, Adela's father,
as a stern young man in 1926.

So reassuring was her voice to me that I was able to pull myself together, dress for school, and have a normal breakfast without letting on that I had heard.

But it bothered me for a long time, and in the many years that have passed I always think of that morning, and then I see a sea of smiling faces, people dancing, Cesar playing his violin, and I hear my mother's voice:

"Casimiro, this room is going to work!"

FERDIE: With the Columbia Restaurant now boasting four dining rooms, and its menu famous because of the contributions of the chef Pijuan and Casimiro, the public began to flood the place. The addition of music and dancing established its prominence, and the motto the extravagant Casimiro I had chosen now became a reality. The Columbia Restaurant had indeed become "The Gem of All Spanish Restaurants."

In 1941 before World War II began, as increasing numbers of locals were becoming regulars and tourists were seeking out the Columbia, a change in management took place that put the finishing touch on the establishment.

Casimiro's brother Lawrence was as open and gregarious as Casimiro was reserved and taciturn. They were as different as day and night, each representing a perfect half of a whole coin. Lawrence had wafted in and out of the Columbia for years, never quite deciding to stay, always seeking his way in outside activities. He sold insurance for a while, was elected justice of the peace, and was appointed head of the county housing and development administration.

Lawrence was a consummate politician, power broker, salesman, and hail-fellow-well-met. Casimiro was comfortable in the kitchen, making shrewd purchases, evaluating the food, inventing new dishes and drinks, taking care of labor-management relations, and in general administering the entire operation like an admiral running a tight ship. It was apparent that they would form a great team, and so the stage was set.

With the war coming on, a boom on the way, and prosperity around the corner, Casimiro and Lawrence agreed it was time to buy out Casimiro's old partner, Manuel Garcia. Lawrence borrowed the funds from several Anglo friends, and the era of Lawrence and Casimiro began. Manuel Garcia moved down Seventh Avenue and took over the highly successful Las Novedades Restaurant, which for years furnished the only real competition the Columbia had in Ybor City.

The two brothers got on exceedingly well because each stayed within his established parameters. Casimiro stayed with the business of business, and Lawrence took care of charisma, public relations, and politics.

During the war years each room of the restaurant filled as soon as the doors opened and stayed packed to capacity until closing. Generals rubbed elbows with senators, a welder from the hills of Kentucky would get drunk next to a boilermaker from Ohio, and entire squadrons from Tampa's MacDill Field would eat their final stateside meals there before getting into their B-17s and pushing into the hostile skies over Europe. For so many it was to be their

The 1905 Bar in the café. The bartender was the highly popular Jesus Fernandez, nicknamed Garrafon (jug).

last memory of home. From Drew Field the fighter pilots would flood into the restaurant, chattering excitedly of the advantages of the P-38 over the P-39 and of the skill of the enemy in Me-109s or Japanese Zeroes. Young people were drinking Bataan royales, or cariocas, or Cuba libres (Cuban Manhattans, which had been invented by Pete the bartender and Casimiro).

During World War II, servicemen sent thousand of letters and cards to the Columbia, but none touched Casimiro as much as a letter from Mike di Bona. He had enclosed a drawing of a large chow hall tent with slab board sides set in the middle of a rock-strewn plain on Le Shima Island. Over the door was a large sign that read: "Columbia Restaurant, Ybor City."

The tent was a mile and a half from where the famous war correspondent Ernie Pyle had died. The shooting had not stopped when Mess Sergeant di Bona set up his chow hall. Japanese air raids and howling windstorms did not stop Sergeant di Bona from serving his Spanish-flavored GI food. Where did he get the ingredients? One source was his grandmother, who sent him bags of Cuban coffee and other ingredients. Ybor City ingenuity and his own creative abilities netted him food with a Columbia flavor. Seventy men of his outfit were Floridians, and they were his greatest fans. Never was a mess sergeant so revered.

Wartime scuttlebutt of a great GI Columbia Restaurant ran through the area, and soon uninvited guests began to appear. Most of them were from Florida or at least had eaten at the real Columbia and came to get di Bona's inventive substitutes and real Cuban coffee.

At the height of its popularity the chow hall was blown apart by a fierce typhoon that swept over the Ryukyus, destroying most of the Okinawa bases and all of Le Shima's Columbia Restaurant.

One of the first buildings rebuilt was made from scrounged plywood sidings, pieces of tent, and iron floor matting. In no time Sergeant di Bona was feeding the wet, miserable men hot Cuban coffee from the Columbia Restaurant, Gem of All Spanish Restaurants, Pacific Division.

Di Bona survived the war and returned to Ybor City and the real Columbia Restaurant. His company of 122 men had periodic reunions at the Columbia but never forgot the home cooking at Mike di Bona's Columbia Restaurant in Le Shima.

For many years the Columbia has hosted the survivors of that brutal air war. First they brought their wives and babies to see the restaurant; then they brought grandchildren or old squadron mates or came alone. They wore faded dark leather pilot's jackets, the painted insignias fading along with the rows of bombs indicating the number of missions they had survived.

They sat alone in the Quixote Room or the Patio, eating garbanzo soup, tasting the splendid chicken and yellow rice, and topping the meal with a fine Tampa cigar and Columbia Cuban coffee. They sat for a long time afterwards, their eyes half closed as the blue smoke curled upward. They seemed to be hearing the squadron voices, as they sang on their last night in the states, at the Columbia:

> We're poor little lambs
> Who have lost our way
> Baa, baa, baa . . .

Lawrence flourished in this atmosphere. In a land of shortages, Lawrence made sure the Columbia had everything, from meat to butter. The Columbia never lacked anything. If ever there was a man at the right place at the right time, it was Lawrence. His office was in the small liquor store behind the café. From there he could keep an eye on the café and receive an endless line of petitioners. Important guests from Washington arrived and came first to see Lawrence at the liquor store. They had to be careful not to compliment Lawrence on a tie or a watch or cuff links. One compliment and Lawrence would give the item to the complimenter. And if the visitors managed to get by that hurdle, Lawrence would give them Chanel No. 5 or silk stockings for their wives.

Lawrence Hernandez, 1944.
Casimiro's younger brother was a master of public relations.

But Lawrence was a man in a hurry to get to the cemetery. He was short and carried too much weight. He was a champion Type A worker, and he seemed to never sleep. He smoked three packs of king-size cigarettes and drank steadily through the day, although I never once saw him drunk.

His passion, aside from power, was his family. He had a strong, dedicated woman behind him in Gloria, who had produced two strong sons. Little Lawrence was a strapping kid with a built-in mean streak, so he was always away at military school. During the war he was sent to Annapolis Naval Academy. Their other son was named Casimiro but called Casey. He was exceedingly handsome and soft and cuddly as a teddy bear. He was sweet and obedi-

Sons of Lawrence at the 1905 Bar, 1947:
Lawrence, Jr. (left), and Casey.

ent, and he too was accepted to Annapolis, but the war ended, relieving him of that difficult task for which he had neither desire nor aptitude.

As 1946 drew to a close, things seemed to be going well for both the family and the restaurant, which was now famous throughout the country. Little Lawrence had graduated, was commissioned, had married, and faced five years of sea duty. Casey was happily enrolled in the University of Maryland. Adela had graduated with honors at Juilliard and was preparing to marry. All pointed to a banner year in 1947.

But, when one abuses the music, the piper takes his toll. Lawrence, on an ever faster treadmill, ignoring his angina pectoris and his doctor's orders, drove himself to an early end. At ten o'clock one morning in December 1946, at the Columbia Café, Lawrence dropped dead of an overwhelming myocardial infarction.

Thus came to an end the halcyon days of the Columbia Restaurant. Now Casimiro faced the sad task of burying his beloved brother and figuring out how to work with his tough nephew Lawrence, who had inherited his father's half.

APPETIZERS AND SNACKS

APERITIVOS Y TAPAS

Black Bean Dip

Caviar de Frijoles Negros

4 cups cooked black beans
 (see p. 34)
4 tablespoons extra-virgin Spanish
 olive oil

4 cloves garlic, crushed
1 onion, chopped
1 hard-boiled egg, chopped
Hot sauce

In a food processor fitted with a steel blade, combine beans and garlic and process until smooth. In a heavy skillet, heat olive oil. Pour black bean puree into skillet, tossing until puree has the consistency of a spread. Season with hot sauce to taste. Cool. Serve in a bowl at room temperature, garnished with chopped onion and chopped egg. Serve with melba toast, saltines, or tiny Cuban crackers.

Black-Eyed Pea Fritters

Bollitos

½ lb. black-eyed peas, dried
4 cloves garlic
2 teaspoons salt

1 teaspoon freshly ground pepper
4 to 6 tablespoons water
Peanut oil or vegetable oil for frying

Rinse black-eyed peas in cold water, pick over to remove foreign particles, and soak overnight in cold water, covered. When peas have softened, remove and discard their skins (just rub them off), soak an additional 30 minutes, drain, and rinse. In a food processor fitted with a steel blade, process peas, garlic, salt, and pepper. With motor running, add the water through the feed tube and continue processing until mixture is smooth and thick.

In large, heavy-bottomed skillet or deep fryer, heat 2 to 3 inches of oil over medium-high heat to 375°, or until a drop of batter sizzles when it touches the oil. Drop mixture by tablespoons into hot oil and fry until golden brown. Drain on paper towels. Serve hot. Makes about 2 dozen fritters.

Chicken Turnovers

Empanadillas de Pollo

Chicken Filling

1 large onion, finely chopped
1 teaspoon chopped garlic
¼ cup extra-virgin olive oil
2 bay leaves
1 8-oz. can tomato sauce
½ cup pimento-stuffed olives,
*   cut in half*

¼ cup raisins
⅛ cup capers
¼ cup cooked chicken, coarsely
*   chopped with knife*
Salt and pepper to taste

Sauté onions in olive oil until limp. Add garlic, tomato sauce, and bay leaves and simmer about 15 minutes. Add chicken and rest of ingredients. Stir well, cover, and cook over low heat for 10 minutes. Cool. This may be made in advance and refrigerated.

Pastry Dough

2 cups all-purpose flour
1 teaspoon salt
⅓ cup shortening
⅓ cup margarine

7 tablespoons ice water
1 egg, lightly beaten
*   with 1 tablespoon water*
*   (for glaze)*

Mix flour and salt. Add shortening and margarine and mix with a fork or pastry blender until mixture resembles coarse cornmeal. Add water, one tablespoon at a time, mixing lightly until dough leaves sides of bowl. Wrap in waxed paper and refrigerate for 30 minutes. Cut dough in half; roll with floured rolling pin into a 10-inch circle. Cut smaller circles with top of a shortening can or any other 4-inch round cutter. (Combine left-over fragments and roll out again.) Repeat with other half of dough.

Make turnovers, putting 1 tablespoon of filling in the center of each circle. Moisten edges with water and fold over. Using fork, crimp edges and prick top twice. Brush with egg-water mixture. Bake in a preheated oven at 400° for 15 minutes or until golden brown. Makes about 16 turn-overs.

*Note: You may also use **picadillo** as the filling (see page 104).*

Codfish Fritters

Frituras de Bacalao

½ lb. salted codfish	½ cup flour
3 tablespoons water	½ teaspoon pepper
1 onion, minced	1 heaping teaspoon baking
2 tablespoons chopped parsley	powder
2 eggs, well beaten	1 clove garlic, minced
½ teaspoon salt	Olive or vegetable oil for frying

Cover codfish with water and soak overnight. Change water 2 or 3 times. Debone codfish and remove dark skin. Shred finely. Beat until light. Add onion, flour, and baking powder. Mix well and add eggs, water, pars-ley, salt, pepper, and garlic. Mix all ingredients thoroughly. Pour enough oil in skillet to deep-fry fritters. With a teaspoon, drop batter into hot oil and fry until golden brown, turning once to fry evenly. Drain fritters on paper towels and serve hot. Makes 18 fritters.

Dates Wrapped in Bacon

Dátiles Envueltos en Tocino

½ lb. thin-sliced bacon, sliced in
  half-strips

1 8-oz. package dates, pitted
Deep fat for frying

Wrap half-slice of bacon around each date. Secure with a toothpick. Fry in deep fat until bacon is light brown. Serves 8.

Eggplant, Marinated Italian Style

Caponata

2 eggplants
3 stalks celery, coarsely chopped
1 onion, finely chopped
¼ cup white wine vinegar
1 tablespoon sugar
1 teaspoon salt

2 tablespoons capers
1 cup green (plain or pimento-
  stuffed) olives, cut in half
1 cup fresh tomatoes, peeled,
  seeded, and chopped
½ cup extra-virgin olive oil

Cut unpeeled eggplants into small cubes. Sprinkle with salt and let stand for one hour. Wash and dry well. Fry eggplant in olive oil and set aside to drain on paper towels. In same oil, sauté onions and celery until limp; add more oil if needed. Add tomatoes, vinegar, sugar, salt, olives, and capers. Add eggplant and simmer for 5 minutes. Cool and serve at room temperature with crackers or melba toast. This will keep in refrigerator for several weeks. Makes 2 quarts.

Fried Ripe Plantains

Plátanos Maduros Fritos

4 ripe plantains, peeled   *Vegetable oil for frying*

Slice plantains diagonally about ½ inch thick. Fry in oil over medium heat, turning to brown on both sides. Drain on paper towels and serve immediately. Serves 6.

Note: Fried plantains may be frozen and reheated in microwave oven when ready to serve.

Ham or Chicken Croquettes

Croquetas de Jamón o Pollo

¼ cup margarine or butter
¼ cup all-purpose flour
1 small to medium onion, minced
1 cup milk
2 eggs
1 tablespoon fresh lemon juice

1½ cups ham or chicken, cooked
* and ground*
Salt and pepper to taste
Fine dry bread crumbs
Peanut oil for frying

Melt butter. Blend in flour, onion, and milk. Cook over medium heat, stirring constantly, until very thick. Stir in 1 egg beaten with lemon juice. Add ham or chicken and salt and pepper to taste. Pour into shallow dish and refrigerate (covered) for 2 hours. Shape into croquettes the size of 3-inch cylinders. Chill. Coat with flour, then dip into mixture of 1 egg beaten with 2 tablespoons water. Roll in crumbs. Deep-fry in hot oil until golden brown. Makes 12 to 16 croquettes.

Oysters or Shrimp Rockefeller

Ostras o Camarones Rockefeller

½ cup parsley leaves, tightly
   packed
1 10-oz. package frozen spinach,
   thawed and drained
4 shallots or 1 small onion
1 tablespoon anise seeds
¾ cup water
¼ teaspoon hot pepper sauce

½ teaspoon celery salt
¼ teaspoon salt
½ teaspoon ground thyme
1 tablespoon anchovy paste
½ cup toasted bread crumbs
½ cup butter or margarine
24 oysters, shucked, or 1 lb. small
   shrimps, peeled and deveined

Put parsley, spinach, and shallots through a food chopper. Simmer anise seed in water for 10 minutes. Strain out seed. Add chopped vegetables to anise-flavored liquid. Simmer, covered, for 10 minutes. Season with pepper sauce, salt, thyme, celery salt, and anchovy paste. Add butter and bread crumbs. Divide oysters or shrimp into 4 individual shells or ramekins. Bake in preheated oven at 350° for about 6 minutes, or broil for 5 minutes. Top each shell or ramekin with a quarter of the spinach mixture and return to broiler for 5 minutes longer. Serves 4.

Plantains Wrapped in Bacon

Plátanos Envueltos en Tocino

4 ripe plantains, peeled
½ lb. sliced bacon

Vegetable or peanut oil for frying

Slice plantains diagonally, about ¾ inch thick. Wrap half a slice of bacon around each plantain slice. Secure bacon with a toothpick. Deep-fry in oil until bacon is brown. Serves 8.

Potatoes in Garlic Mayonnaise

Papas Ali-oli

2 lbs. Red Bliss potatoes
1 cup mayonnaise
2 tablespoons extra-virgin
   olive oil

1 tablespoon garlic, finely minced
   or pressed
Salt and pepper
Chopped parsley

Boil potatoes in their jackets until tender. Drain, peel, and cut into thick slices. Mix mayonnaise, olive oil, and garlic until smooth. Combine with potatoes until they are well coated. Salt and pepper to taste. Garnish with chopped parsley. Serves 4 to 6.

Russian Salad

Ensaladilla Rusa

4 medium potatoes, boiled,
   peeled, and diced
¼ cup cooked carrots, diced
¼ cup frozen green peas,
   cooked
2 tablespoons rice vinegar
2 tablespoons olive oil

Salt and pepper to taste
¾ cup mayonnaise
1 clove garlic, crushed
1 6½-oz. can solid white albacore
   tuna, flaked
Pimento or roasted red pepper
   strips

Mix potatoes, carrots, and peas. In a separate bowl, mix oil, vinegar, salt, and pepper. Add tuna. Combine mayonnaise and garlic and fold into tuna mixture. Fold in vegetables. Refrigerate. Allow to come to room temperature before serving. Decorate with pimento strips. Serves 4 to 6.

Seafood Croquettes

Croquetas de Mariscos

1 stick butter	2 tablespoons dry white wine
1 medium onion, chopped fine	½ lb. shrimps, cooked and
1 cup flour	chopped
2 cups milk, heated	½ lb. lobster, cooked and
2 eggs, beaten lightly	chopped
¼ teaspoon nutmeg	½ lb. cooked crabmeat, flaked
½ teaspoon Tabasco sauce	Salt and pepper

Melt butter in skillet. Sauté onion until transparent. Add flour and stir until it forms a ball with butter and onion. Add hot milk and stir until mixture becomes a thick sauce. Beat eggs with nutmeg, Tabasco, and wine. Fold into cream sauce; add salt and pepper to taste. Add seafood and mix thoroughly. Cover and chill.

CROQUETTE PREPARATION

2 eggs, beaten lightly	Vegetable or peanut oil for frying
Bread crumbs	Flour

Using a tablespoon and floured hands, divide and form seafood mixture into cylinder shapes. Roll each croquette in flour, dip in egg, and coat with bread crumbs. Chill for about 1 hour. Fry in hot oil 1½ inches deep, turning croquette until golden. Drain. Makes 36.

Spanish Bean Soup Dip

Dip de Potaje de Garbanzos

1 quart Spanish bean soup
  (see p. 48)
¼ cup olive oil

1 hard-boiled egg, chopped
⅓ cup parsley, chopped
Tabasco sauce

Puree Spanish bean soup. Heat oil in skillet. Add puree to skillet and cook over medium heat until mushy. Season with Tabasco sauce to taste. Cool. Serve in a deep bowl garnished with chopped egg and parsley. Melba toast goes well with this dip.

Spanish Pickled Kingfish

Serrucho en Escabeche

3 lbs. kingfish, cut in 1-inch-thick
  round steaks
4 large onions, cut in thin slices
4 green peppers, cut in strips
3 bay leaves
10 cloves garlic, crushed
½ teaspoon Spanish or Hungarian
  paprika

12 black peppercorns
1 cup pitted green olives
1 cup white wine vinegar
2 cups extra-virgin olive oil
Flour for dredging fish
Salt and pepper to taste

Salt and pepper fish; dredge in flour. In 1 cup olive oil, fry until golden. Remove fish from frying pan and set aside; when cool, remove large bones. Strain oil just used, return to pan, and add the other cup of oil. Sauté onions, green peppers, bay leaves, and garlic until limp. Add paprika, peppercorns, olives, and vinegar. In a glass, china, or clay casserole, place layer of fried fish, then layer of vegetable mixture. Repeat layering several times; the last layer should be the vegetable mixture. Cover and refrigerate. Will keep for a week or 10 days. Serves 6 to 8.

Spanish Pickled Shrimp

Camarones en Escabeche

2 lbs. shrimps, peeled and deveined

3 large onions, cut in thin slices

3 green peppers, cut in strips

2 bay leaves

8 cloves garlic, crushed

½ teaspoon Spanish or Hungarian paprika

10 black peppercorns

¾ cup green olives, pitted

¾ cup white wine vinegar

1½ cups extra-virgin olive oil

Salt and pepper

Heat oil in skillet. Sauté onions, green peppers, bay leaves, and garlic until onion is transparent. Add shrimp and cook over medium heat for 2 minutes. Add paprika, olives, peppercorns, and vinegar. Mix and add salt and pepper to taste. Transfer to glass, china, or clay casserole. Cover and refrigerate. Will keep for a week or 10 days. Serves 8.

Spinach Balls

Bolitas de Espinacas

2 10-oz. packages frozen chopped
   spinach
¾ cup melted butter or margarine
3 cups herb-seasoned stuffing mix
½ cup grated Parmesan cheese
1 tablespoon pepper

1 large onion, finely chopped
1½ teaspoons finely minced
   garlic
6 medium eggs, well beaten
1½ teaspoons garlic salt
½ teaspoon thyme

Thaw and drain spinach. Squeeze to remove excess moisture. Combine spinach and remaining ingredients and mix well. Shape mixture into ¾-inch balls and place on lightly greased cookie sheet. Bake at 325° for 20 minutes. Makes 11 dozen.

Stuffed Mashed Potato Balls

Papas Rellenas

2 lbs. potatoes, peeled
Salt and freshly ground black pepper
1 cup **picadillo** (see p. 104)

1 large egg, lightly beaten
½ cup bread crumbs
Peanut or vegetable oil for frying

In a large pot, cook potatoes, covered in salted water, until tender, 20 to 25 minutes. Drain. Place them back in the pot until all moisture has evaporated. Puree or mash until smooth. Season with salt and pepper to taste. Allow potatoes to rest 30 minutes at room temperature.

Shape pureed potatoes into 3-inch balls. Make a well in each ball with a spoon, fill with 1 tablespoon of *picadillo*, and then reshape into a ball. Roll the balls first in beaten egg and then in bread crumbs. Place on a platter, cover, and refrigerate 1 hour. In large heavy-bottomed skillet or deep fryer, heat 2 to 3 inches of oil to 375°. Fry the balls 2 or 3 at a time until golden brown on all sides, turning with a slotted spoon. Drain on a paper-lined platter. Serve hot. Serves 8.

Water Chestnut Meatballs

Albóndigas de Castañas Orientales

2 cups soft bread crumbs
½ lb. pork sausage
½ lb. ground beef
1 8-oz. can water chestnuts,
    drained and chopped

1 tablespoon soy sauce
¼ teaspoon onion powder
½ teaspoon garlic salt
½ cup milk
1 16-oz. can sweet-and-sour sauce

Combine all ingredients except sweet-and-sour sauce. Mix well and shape in 1-inch balls. Place in greased pan or dish. Bake at 350° for 25 to 30 minutes. Add sauce and mix lightly to coat meatballs. Bake additional 15 minutes. Makes about 4 dozen meatballs.

DRINKS

✸

BEBIDAS

Bataan Royale

½ oz. gin
½ oz. lime juice
½ oz. cherry liqueur
5 dashes grenadine

½ oz. white rum
3 dashes triple sec
Orange slice

Mix all ingredients and shake. Serve in large wine glass over ice, garnished with orange slice. Serves 1.

Carioca

1 oz. white rum
¼ oz. lemon juice
1 oz. pineapple juice

2 dashes Amer Picon liqueur
1 tablespoon sugar

Shake all ingredients together with ice and serve in tall tulip glass. Serves 1.

Champion

1 oz. passion fruit juice
1 oz. bourbon
1 oz. grapefruit juice

1 oz. white rum
¼ oz. lemon juice
Mint leaves

Shake in blender. Serve in collins glass over ice, garnished with mint leaves. Serves 1.

Cuba Libre

1½ ounces white rum
Juice of ¼ lime or lemon
4 ice cubes

Cola
1 maraschino cherry

Stir rum and lime juice together in chilled highball glass. Add ice cubes, pour cola to fill glass, and stir. Garnish with cherry. Serves 1.

Daiquiri

2 ounces white Bacardi rum
1 tablespoon sugar
1 teaspoon maraschino liqueur

1 teaspoon grapefruit juice
Juice of half a lemon
½ cup crushed ice

Mix all ingredients, shake well, and strain into martini glass or champagne flute. Serves 1.

Note: This special recipe is from the Floridita Bar in Havana.

Havana Cooler

2 ounces white rum
1 teaspoon lemon juice
1 teaspoon pineapple juice
1 teaspoon maraschino cherry juice

1 teaspoon orange juice
Dash orange bitters
Fruit for garnish

Combine rum, juices, and bitters. Shake well with ice and strain into highball glass filled with ice. Garnish with lemon slices (or orange) and cherry. (Pineapple stick is also attractive, if available). Serves 1.

Mojito

Several sprigs of mint
Juice of 1 lemon
1 teaspoon sugar
2 ounces rum

1 strip of lemon peel
Cracked ice
Soda water

Using an 8-oz. glass, mull mint with sugar. Add rest of ingredients and stir. Add ice and soda water to fill glass. Serves 1.

Presidente Cocktail

½ oz. sweet vermouth
Dash Amer Picon liqueur
½ oz. dry vermouth
1 maraschino cherry

1 oz. gold rum
Dash grenadine
Lemon peel

Stir wet ingredients in cocktail shaker. Add lemon peel and cherry. Serve over ice in old-fashioned glass or martini glass. Serves 1.

Sangria

1 bottle red wine, Spanish
    (preferably from Rioja)
¼ cup brandy
2 tablespoons lemon juice
2 tablespoons orange juice

1 tablespoon sugar
1 cup club soda
Orange slices
Maraschino cherries

Mix all ingredients (except orange slices and cherries) in a large pitcher. Stir with a wooden spoon until well mixed. Pour into large wine glasses. Garnish with orange slices and cherries.

If desired, you may add ice to pitcher. Serves 4.

Silver Meteor

1 oz. white rum   ½ oz. Cointreau
1 oz. orange juice

Stir ingredients together in mixing glass. Serve over ice in tall champagne flute. Serves 1.

Chapter Five

THE COLUMBIA
FAMILY

FERDIE: When the Columbia Restaurant reached its highest point of critical and financial success, during World War II, its owners found that they had done more than blend a team of experts; they had bonded into the Columbia family.

The mark of success of a business in those days—when pride in one's work counted, when pride of ownership and a good employee-employer relationship were criteria to be valued—was a corps of happy employees. The Columbia Restaurant boasted a family of long-term employees who made the restaurant great and who stayed employed until their deaths.

The most important employee a restaurant has is the cook. A master chef is indispensable for creating a good reputation and maintaining it. In 1941 Admiral Chester W. Nimitz of the United States Navy said, "Give me a good cook and I'll show you a first-rate aircraft carrier. Give me four good cooks and I'll beat the Japanese fleet at Midway." And we all know how Midway turned out. The other side of that coin is best illustrated by the skimpy fare served on the *Bounty*. A bad cook equals mutiny.

The Columbia Restaurant was fortunate indeed to have discovered a royal master chef. Francisco Pijuan, known simply as Pijuan, came from the kitchens of the royal family of King Alfonso XIII of Spain. He brought to the Columbia a mastery never before imagined in Ybor City. His kitchen was his domain, and he ruled it with an iron hand. Consistency of excellence was his byword. His secret was that he considered his profession to be of the highest

The master chef Pijuan (center) in his domain, 1943.

order. He was a high priest of the culinary art, and he practiced on the altar of the hearth, stove, and oven.

Pijuan started cooking in Spain when he was fourteen years old. He joined the cooking staff of a captain general and then was shifted to the kitchen of Alfonso XIII. Pijuan remembered the king as a man of simple tastes who liked garbanzo soup, *olla* (garbanzo soup with cabbage), *cordero estofado* (lamb stew), and a dish called *callos andaluza,* a stew of tripe with garbanzos.

When he left the service of the king he migrated to Cuba, and in 1923, conveniently overlooking immigration restrictions, smuggled himself into Tarpon Springs, Florida. Casimiro I had a nose for talent and hired him for the Columbia, where he worked until he died.

He was a short, stocky man with a ruddy face and a truculent expression. He was the absolute master of all he surveyed. He uttered orders to his various helpers in a mumble, and a look from him could paralyze even the most seasoned cook or expert waiter.

In Pijuan's day, nothing was frozen, automated, or written down. The dozens of waiters would come to the counter and wait for Pijuan to look at them. "One steak Pijuan, medium. One steak *criolla*, rare. One pompano *papillot*. And *arroz con pollo* for six." Pijuan would nod, indicating it was recorded in his computer brain. Woe betide the man who ordered incorrectly! Better to dump the order in the clothes hamper than to return to the kitchen with an incorrect order. If, for example, a customer wanted a medium steak and the waiter had ordered well-done, there was no saving it. Best dump it and order a new one. To admit the mistake was to get chased out of the kitchen at a dead run.

Pijuan's inordinate pride in his product led him to watch the plates as they returned. Was it all gone? Had they left some uneaten? When things were slow in the kitchen, Pijuan would peek out to see the look on the customers' faces. Once a tourist ordered his prized steak Pijuan. Then he asked for a bottle of ketchup and Tabasco sauce. Pijuan turned red, stomped out, and withdrew the plate from the startled customer. "Go and eat at Morrison's Cafeteria," he said.

My personal disaster as a waiter came when, in a spasm of overconfidence, I tried to carry five plates of spaghetti and meatballs on one arm. It was late in the day, and I was trying to imitate the way the fancy waiters swung their arms as they turned the corners.

I came steaming out of the kitchen, took a nice banking turn, swinging the dishes in an arc, and watched the red, slippery spaghetti splat on the tile floor with a sickening sound. My white apron was now a beautiful red. The few patrons in La Fonda and the waiters folding napkins at the back round table broke out into loud laughter. Not only did I have to clean up the mess, but worst of all, I had to go back to the kitchen and reorder five spaghetti dishes from Pijuan!

I had not counted on the solidarity and love of the Columbia family. My Aunt Lola was the first, main, and longest-employed cashier. My father, J.B., was intimately associated with Lawrence and a great friend of Casimiro. I was regarded as a pet. Mine was a summer job. Everyone knew I was going off to college to become a doctor.

"Five orders of spaghetti and meatballs?" Pijuan said mildly, taking a huge bite out of a head of lettuce. I nodded, knowing he was letting me off the hook. Not another word was said about it, then or ever, by Pijuan, who despite his feared persona was a softie at heart.

ADELA: *I remember one year my father and Pijuan decided on a nice publicity stunt. They would go to the state fair and buy whatever heifer won the first prize at the livestock exhibit.*

Pepin the headwaiter, Pijuan, and my daddy bought the winner for $1,200. The picture appeared in the paper the next day, and Pijuan repaired to his kitchen, ready to fix his great variety of steak dishes for the expected overflow crowd.

But the first customer who appeared that morning was the man who had sold the prize heifer. With him was his young son, red-faced and sobbing. Hurriedly the man told my father that the heifer had been the pet of his son since it was born. He offered to pay back the money.

Touched by the crying boy, my father quickly called the slaughterhouse. Unfortunately, it was too late, and the disconsolate pair left the restaurant, turning down my father's offer of a free Columbia lunch.

FERDIE: It's a little ironic that the two dishes that helped to make the Columbia famous are actually French dishes.

Pompano *en papillot* and steak capuchina were first introduced in Paris, thence to Spain and Cuba, and finally to Ybor City, where Pijuan added his special twist. In the heyday of the Columbia, during the long reign of Pijuan and later Sarapico, the restaurant used fifty thousand sheets of heavy paper. The sheets were twelve by eighteen inches, folded and trimmed with scissors to round off the edges. The chief purpose of the paper (*papillot*) is to provide a miniature oven, which encloses the meat or fish and helps the dish to retain all its natural juices and flavors.

There were the inevitable "secrets" of the kitchen. Pijuan maintained that if you want a steak "medium," you cook it in the paper "rare." The heat retained by the paper after the steak is off the stove cooks the meat for a few moments more. Novice cooks, unaware of this factor, find themselves with overcooked steaks.

ADELA: *Pompano **en papillot** (shortened on our menu to "pompano papillot") is a complicated dish. The fish is boned and filleted, cut in half, and put*

A great publicity stunt turned sad. Left to right: Pepin the headwaiter, the prize cow, and Pijuan, ready to start work.

on a piece of buttered paper with layers of seafood dressing. The paper is folded over, and the dish is baked in the oven at 475°. The degree of brown to which the paper turns indicates when it is done.

When we first started, my father would send the waiters to the table with the paper bag untouched, leaving the customer to remove it. To his horror, he found that many customers ate the paper, which, being soaked in butter and gravy, was flavorful.

One customer wrote my father praising the pompano papillot, noting at the end, "I particularly liked the crust." At that point it was decided to let the waiter remove the paper at tableside and serve the pompano.

*At one time the Columbia boasted various "paper" dishes. Steak capuchina, chicken papillot, lamb chops papillot, called **ville rue,** and other meats in paper were on the menu. But today only the pompano papillot remains on the menu.*

Pijuan was a special favorite of my father, who appreciated genius wherever he found it. Only once in Pijuan's many years as chef did my father come close to losing him.

Although Pijuan had slipped into the country, my family had been able to legitimize his stay through political connections. The problem came when Pijuan insisted on bringing in his wife and son. They were denied entrance, and Pijuan told Daddy that if they could not join him, he was quitting to return to Cuba and his family.

By then Uncle Lawrence had political pull in Washington, and he and my daddy went to work. The Congressional Record now shows Private Law 225, "For the relief of Mrs. Pacios Pijuan," which allowed her to join her husband in America. Such is the power of pompano papillot.

FERDIE: When Pijuan died, his will specified that he be buried holding a Columbia menu in his crossed arms. Casimiro II saw to it that his request was granted. After the funeral, he immediately set out to find someone worthy of wearing Pijuan's chef's hat.

He did not have far to look. He found him right under his nose at the Columbia.

Vincenzo Perez was a small, nervous man, whose darting about and short, rapid bursts of energy earned him the nickname "Sarapico," which means "little bird," like a sand crane. In Ybor City, then as now, once a nickname sticks, it is the name by which you are known. Everyone knows Sarapico. Few know his real name.

Sarapico has had a long and varied career. Starting as a busboy, then working as a waiter, and finally as a chef, he worked in New York in a Jewish kosher restaurant, then an American diner, a Chinese restaurant, an Italian café, and finally at the Spanish Pavilion.

Few chefs will disclose the secrets of their art, and Sarapico is no different. The little twists that make the difference between an appetizing dish and a poorly prepared one are learned through years of experience. Sarapico obtained his culinary secrets from a score of cooks in all types of restaurants. But he revealed to us a few tricks that might help cooks preparing meals at home.

There's burned spaghetti sauce. If by some mischance you've forgotten to stir the simmering spaghetti sauce and you discover some of the sauce

Sarapico, successor to Pijuan, and his paella, 1950.

charred on the bottom of the pan, don't be discouraged. The whole sauce isn't ruined. To remove the burnt taste, just put several slices of bread in the sauce. Somehow the yeast soaks up the burnt taste and leaves the sauce as palatable as before.

Bread also comes in handy for keeping cauliflower white. Before he learned that trick, Sarapico's cauliflower sometimes turned a sorrowful yellow or pink, according to the way it was prepared. But a Japanese chef showed him how to place ordinary bread in the pot with cauliflower, and it always comes out snow white.

Then there is the mishap of a pan of deep fat catching fire. The Columbia chefs keep baking soda close by for such an emergency. If the flame cannot be extinguished by covering the pan, a mixture of soda and water poured into the pan quickly extinguishes it. This ordinarily would ruin the grease for further use. But here again, Sarapico has a trick. Put bread into the grease, and the bread will soak up the soda, leaving the fat free of any strange taste.

If beans, dried or fresh, should become hard during cooking, Sarapico has a simple device for tenderizing. He just puts a nail into the pot, and somehow, the beans become tender.

In 1937 Sarapico started as a waiter at the Fonda. When I worked there, I knew him as a fast-moving, hard-driving, possessed waiter, covered with sweat and looking like he was working harder than any other waiter. While preparing this book I talked to Serafin, a waiter who stayed at the Columbia for thirty years and who is best known as the father of Bob Martinez, former governor of Florida. Serafin noted, "Sarapico was a wonderful chef but a bad waiter because his legs and arms were too short. No matter how fast he ran he couldn't cover the same distance as the King, who walked slow. And the other thing was he talked too much to the customers."

This amused me no end since I remember Serafin as a body clone of Sarapico. They both were short, thick of body, with short arms and legs. And Serafin was a top-notch waiter. During the war Serafin held two full-time jobs. His work in the Two Brothers Dairy was considered "essential for the war effort" and so earned him a deferment to stay home. Since dairy work is an early morning job, he was able to keep his full-time Columbia job. It was a killing schedule, which he kept up for four years. At times I thought he would have been safer in the army.

Casimiro's judgment proved correct once again, for Sarapico took command of the kitchen and did not relinquish the helm until 1968, when he left to become a chef/partner in a steakhouse.

ADELA: *My husband, Cesar, who had not been around during Pijuan's time, loved Sarapico. He and my father bought Sarapico a house and helped him educate his son and daughter. My daddy, however, held that the great Pijuan had no peer. I have a photo of Daddy, Cesar, and Sarapico at a banquet that proves a picture is indeed worth a thousand words. In it, Cesar holds up two fingers indicating that the Columbia has boasted two great chefs. Sarapico accepts the praise. Look closely and you see Daddy making a face and holding up one finger. There was only one master chef at the Columbia Restaurant as far as Daddy was concerned.*

Cesar Gonzmart holds up two fingers to show that there had been two great chefs at the Columbia. Casimiro holds up one finger, indicating that there was only one: Pijuan. Left to right: Adela (seated), Pete the bartender, Casimiro, Sarapico, and Cesar, 1961.

FERDIE: My maiden aunt, Lola Jimenez, became a legendary fixture at the Columbia cash register, which was located at the front, between the coffee shop and La Fonda.

From that vantage point her hawk eyes surveyed the restaurant. Her record of never having missed a day and never having been late is unmatched to this day. Her accuracy was the topic of conversation among the employees. One New Year's Eve she could not balance her register and was short by twenty-five cents. Entreaties by Casimiro and Lawrence fell on deaf ears. She stayed until she had found all but a two-penny discrepancy.

Once, two workmen showed up with tools to break up the tiles around the

A bevy of costumed beauties in a publicity photo, 1939. Lola, the cashier, in her
Mexican patriotic finery, is second from right; Adela is third from right.

front of the cashier's station. One waiter, on being asked what was happening,
made a comment that became the running joke at the Columbia: "Oh, Lola
dropped a dime and it got lost in the cracks, so she's tearing up the tiles to
find it."

She lived next to my house on Lamar Street, and I loved her dearly, for she
was my second mother, who spoiled me and who taught me to drive when
I was twelve in her spotless, brand-new 1939 Plymouth. Her car was her
pride and joy, and she drove it only to work and back. She kept it in a garage
at the Columbia as well as at her house, so the car never got wet. When she
died, it had such low mileage that people thought she had fixed the speedom-
eter. Imagine her anguish as she let me drive her car on the narrow streets of
Ybor City.

She was serious and very conservative, yet on one day of the year she
seemed to take leave of her senses. On Mexican Independence Day in Septem-
ber she would dress in a loud Mexican costume, with serape, beads, and a
crazy hat, and go to work at the Columbia. Casimiro II must have fainted
when she first showed up in this garish, exotic dress. But Lola didn't seem to

notice if anyone stared, for with her it was business first. I can remember hiding under my house so I wouldn't be teased by my gang about my crazy Aunt Lola in her strange Mexican dress.

While Lola lived, Casimiro never had to worry about the cash. She trained new cashiers who proved capable, but none ever attained the reputation for fearsome accuracy that Lola did.

Even though she had a rheumatic heart with valvular damage and she was ordered to quit work, she would not. Her loyalty to the Columbia was boundless. She worked until she died. You might say she balanced her tape perfectly in life. The Columbia was her life, and she would not leave it.

✥ Gregorio Martinez came to Tampa in the early 1920s and took a job in the speakeasy across the street from the Columbia. He was working one night when the federals raided the place. Terrified of being arrested and deported, Gregorio ran to the restroom and squeezed through the window. Now he was out on the street but still wearing his waiter's outfit.

Mindful that he stood out like a sore thumb, he ran into the Columbia Café and started waiting on tables. A bemused Casimiro I, watching the frantic new waiter, deduced his problem. Seeing that he was a first-rate waiter, Casimiro offered him a job. As the days passed, Gregorio grew a mustache in a misguided notion that it would fool the federals.

With a mustache, he bore a startling resemblance to Alfonso XIII of Spain. Casimiro began calling him El Rey, the King, and that moniker stuck on him for life. He was the first of the great waiters of the Columbia.

A D E L A: *My daddy had become discouraged with the way things were going during the Depression, with financial disaster staring him in the face. My grandfather, Viejo, had left him a stack of bills and unpaid debts that seemed insurmountable.*

One day, when the cash receipts had added up to $12.50 for the entire twenty-four-hour period, my father gave the King the money and told him to go buy some plywood to nail over the doors. "If business continues this bad," he said, "I'm closing up the place."

The King said nothing and left. He stayed gone a long time, and when he came back he put $503 on the table. He had drawn out his entire savings.

Gregorio Martinez (El Rey, the King), master waiter at work, 1946.

"Don't close the place," said the King simply. My father didn't know what to say. He didn't take the money, but he didn't close the place either, and he made a vow that as long as he lived, the King would have employment at the Columbia.

FERDIE: The King was in great demand. Not only was he capable of elegant service, but talking to him in English was an adventure not to be missed, for he was convinced that he spoke English as well as anyone. On second thought, if "anyone" referred to the staff of the Columbia, he might well have been right.

He taught me several key pointers on being a first-rate professional waiter. First thing was to never be in a hurry. He did things deliberately, walked at a regal pace, and never made a mistake. The second thing was never to walk anywhere without something in your hand: no wasted trips. In the café, where we had to clean our own tables, this was an invaluable tip. Lastly, he said to be unfailingly polite and to act as if you had heard nothing at the table but their order. This also proved an invaluable tip when I found myself waiting on mafiosi, politicians, bankers, and their ilk. People say the damnedest things in front of waiters.

The King worked as a headwaiter until arthritis crippled him, and he retired with an enviable record of longevity.

When I write of a measured, stately walk I think of two other waiters, Ramonin Lopez and Evaristo. Both stayed with the Columbia for a long time, but Ramonin stayed for forty years and worked until he was in his eighties. His son Ray Lopez became one of the eminent neurologists of our state.

A D E L A : *There were so many who served and stayed for long years. Names like El Curro, Jarruco, Luis, Cuatro Pelos, the Great Roche, Luis Cabello, and so many, many more. All characters, all waiters who took their calling as a profession. Maybe that is why they were so good.*

The Columbia Café waiters in particular were a different breed. They had to do it all. No busboys, no help from any quarter, and it was a track meet for eight solid hours. Men like Eddie Piñeiro, Miguel, Lamela, Ramón, and Bebe Menendez were highly regarded by their peers.

F E R D I E : Pete Scaglione, the head bartender, was totally bald and had a beautifully shaped head. He seldom smiled or spoke. He was a machine of efficiency. He was a skipper in command of his boat. The entire restaurant was his domain. He tolerated no mischief, and he safeguarded the place as if it were his own. Between Lola and Pete, woe betide any customer or employee trying to pull a fast one on the Columbia.

I called him the Enforcer because he enforced the rules of the house and backed up waiters in disputes with customers. Once Jimmy Longo, Santo Trafficante's trusted lieutenant, came in with a bag containing two freshly made guava pastries from the bakery across the street. He ordered his usual coffee, which I served promptly. He pulled out the two guava pastries and asked for the bill. Pete got hold of me as I put my pad on the bar.

"How much are you charging Jimmy?"

"A dime for coffee?" I asked, knowing what was coming.

Pete Scaglione, watchdog of the Columbia and inventive mixologist, 1957.

"How much for the pastries?" Pete fixed me with a hard stare.

"But . . ." I did not want to argue with Pete.

"We sell pastries here. Twenty cents plus a dime for coffee."

When Jimmy Longo saw the bill he started to say something; then he looked behind me. There was Pete, as square and solid as the Rock of Gibraltar. Quietly he pulled out a quarter and a dime, smiled, and walked away. My tip was a nickel, and my life was spared.

Pete kept a small bat behind the bar. He never had to use it, to my knowledge. He really didn't need to, for one look at Pete's face told you all you needed to know.

ADELA: *He was so devoted to my father that it was touching to me. My father returned his devotion, and from time to time they would get together and invent new drinks.*

My father never owned a car until 1940, when he was reasonably sure he could afford one. He bought a blue 1940 Chevrolet Deluxe, four doors, with a vacuum stick shift. It was his first car, and he bought it because he was building a house too far from the Columbia to walk to work.

In the 1950s he decided to get a new car, and he gave the Chevrolet to Pete. To Pete it was as if he had been awarded the Congressional Medal of Honor. In spite of the fact that it was twelve years old, it was still like new.

FERDIE: Joe Fernandez (Pepin) was a handsome and eccentric man, a top headwaiter in any league.

A political crony of Lawrence, he had been brought in to handle the door when the overflow crowds began to appear during the war years. He had been a health inspector, which left him with a lifelong fear of germs. He hated germs so much that he washed the lettuce and tomatoes with soap before eating them.

He possessed a politician's memory for names. The bigger the tipper, the louder Pepin would announce his name. "Oh, Mr. Witt, how are you tonight!" he would bellow so that they heard him in the deepest recesses of the wine cellar. "And how beautiful you look tonight, Mrs. Witt," he would coo, a few decibels lower. He would march them by waiting lines of tourists and servicemen and proceed to a choice table, pocketing the folded bill effortlessly.

The waiters called him Cabeza Vocina (loudspeaker head) and laughed, but they all liked him and admired the way he handled the door. After all, the happier the customer is when he bypasses the lines and sits at a choice table, the better the chance of a fat tip.

Pepin was also good with children and teens, paying special attention to toddlers, walking them over to see the fountain, surprising them with a cherry on a toothpick.

But he was an unusual man. He drove a shambling wreck of a 1930 Model A. The driver's door latch was nonexistent, and he had to tie the door with a piece of rope. In 1945 Lawrence gave him his big luxurious 1941 Chrysler. Pepin loved the gesture, hated the car. It wasn't him. After a month of making a great show of driving it to work, he slyly began alternating with the Model A, using the lame excuse that gas rationing did not allow him to feed the gas-guzzling Chrysler. Eventually the Chrysler became a permanent resident of his garage, and Pepin continued blissfully in his Model A.

He worked until illness forced him to quit after four decades as the voice of the Columbia. His gentlemanly elegance was greatly missed after he retired, and no more could the customers enjoy hearing the ringing announcement of their arrival, no more would children play at the fountain, nor lovers hide in a romantic dark corner. The Columbia had lost a distinctive voice.

🍃 Dance music arrived at the Columbia in 1936, and with it came a young piano man. In his photo he looks absurdly young, a handsome kid not old enough to work in a club.

Henry Tudela, gentle, perennial pianist, with the original Don Quixote band in 1936. He started that year and is still playing at the Columbia.

Today, you step into the Siboney Room (named after the 1920s hit song by Cuban composer Ernesto Lecuona), and a man sits at the piano who bears a faint resemblance to the callow youth of the photograph of 1938. This man looks too old to be up this late playing for dancing and dining.

Henry Tudela was a sharp, handsome kid with an ear for jazz and fast fingers to play it. When he left for a stint in the army, Tudela got a taste for life in the big cities of the North, where jazz could be heard, where a kid could play the kind of music he cared for.

It appeared that Tudela would go back up north when he was discharged from the army in 1945. He came home to get some money and a few suits out of the cleaners, and before he could say "Duke Ellington," forty-nine years had passed and he was still playing at the Siboney in the Columbia.

I remember sitting with this vibrant young man in the café between sets and talking jazz. He spoke reverentially about a blind black pianist named Art Tatum who played complicated solos with blinding speed and about a white jazz man named Lenny Tristano whose advanced music was revolutionizing jazz. Heady stuff to hear. After all, Tudela had been there. He had heard the music of Fifty-second Street in New York. He was on his way.

But first he had to stop by the cellar of the Centro Asturiano and play some gin rummy with J.B., or maybe a hand or two of hearts with Al Lopez, Tomate, Pelusa, and the old guys. And then, before he knew it, it was time to get in his tux and play "Siboney" for the tourists in the Quixote Room or play show music for the floor show.

Time passed him by. He sits stooped at the keyboard, playing in his precise way the thousands of tunes he banked in his memory. He's had a myriad of health problems. He married Tomate's widow, the beautiful Toby, and she is also burdened with illness.

Sometimes I look at him, bent over the keyboard, ashes on the front of his tux, and I wonder if he hears the chords of "How High the Moon," if he hears the elegant notes of Duke Ellington's "Prelude to a Kiss," and if he sometimes wonders how it is that he somehow forgot to get back to Fifty-second Street and the possibility of playing with Bird and Dizzy and Miles.

So . . . play it again, Henry,
Play it one more time for me, Henry,
Play "Siboney."

MEATS

✽

CARNES

Beef Stew with Potatoes, Spanish Style

Carne con Papas

*1 lb. tenderloin of beef tips,
    trimmed and cut in 1-inch
    cubes*
½ teaspoon sweet paprika
1 green pepper, chopped
*1 cup canned whole tomatoes,
    chopped*
1 onion, chopped

2 tablespoons olive oil
*3 medium potatoes, peeled and
    cut in 1½-inch chunks*
1 bay leaf
2 cloves garlic, minced
*Pimento or roasted red pepper
    strips and green peas (cooked)
    for garnish*

Brown beef tips in oil. When half-cooked, add green pepper, onion, bay leaf, garlic, and paprika. Cook with tomatoes over medium heat for 15 minutes. Place potatoes with meat and tomato mixture in casserole dish, and bake for 40 minutes at 350°. Decorate with peas and pimento strips. Serves 3.

Brisket of Beef

Pecho de Vaca Estofada

6 to 7 lb. brisket of beef
4 large onions, sliced
8 cloves garlic, minced
¼ cup ketchup

3 tablespoons vegetable oil
Salt and pepper to taste
¼ cup burgundy

Brown brisket over medium heat in oil, in a heavy frying pan. Lower heat and paint beef with ketchup on both sides. Spread half the onions in bottom of frying pan and put beef on top. Cover with remaining onions and garlic. Add wine, salt, and pepper and cover tightly. Cook for approximately 2½ hours over very low heat. Remove meat from pan and pour juices and onions into a blender or food processor. Puree until smooth. Cut beef in thin slices and arrange in a baking dish. Pour gravy over meat, cover with foil, and warm in oven. This may be served with boiled potatoes that have been browned in the oven with some of the gravy from the brisket. Serves 8.

Cuban Beef Hash

Picadillo

2 lbs. lean boneless beef (preferably chuck), trimmed of excess fat and ground

4 tablespoons vegetable oil

1 cup onions, finely chopped

2 teaspoons garlic, minced

2 large green peppers, finely chopped

1 teaspoon oregano

2 teaspoons salt

Freshly ground pepper to taste

4 bay leaves

6 medium-size firm ripe tomatoes, peeled, seeded, and finely chopped (or 2 cups canned whole tomatoes, drained and chopped)

½ teaspoon ground cumin

½ cup small pimento-stuffed green olives

¼ cup seedless raisins

1 tablespoon white vinegar

¼ cup burgundy

In a 10- to 12-inch skillet, heat oil over medium heat until a light haze forms above it. Sauté onions and peppers, stirring frequently, for about 5 minutes, or until vegetables are soft but not brown. Add tomatoes and garlic. Still stirring, cook briskly until most of the liquid in the pan has evaporated. Add ground beef, oregano, bay leaves, and cumin. Stir until meat is no longer red. Add salt, pepper, vinegar, raisins, olives, and wine. Cook at low temperature for approximately 15 minutes. Traditionally *picadillo* is served with fluffy white rice and, when available, fried ripe plantains. Serves 4–6.

Cuban Sandwich

Sandwich Cubano

10-inch loaf of Cuban bread
4 thin slices smoked ham
2 thin slices fresh pork ham
2 slices Genoa salami, cut in half

2 slices Swiss cheese
3 sour pickle slices (may also use
  dill)
Yellow mustard

Slice bread down middle lengthwise. Layer ingredients to cover bottom half of bread in the following order: ham, pork, salami, cheese, and pickles. Spread mustard on top half of bread. Cover bottom half and slice sandwich diagonally. Sandwich may be heated in oven or served at room temperature. If Cuban bread is not available, you may use French bread (baguette type) or Italian bread.

Cuban Stuffed Pot Roast

———— ❧ ————

Boliche Relleno

3 lbs. **boliche** (*eye round of beef*)
1 large green pepper, cut in strips
3 large onions, sliced in half-moons
2 tablespoons oregano
4 bay leaves
6 cloves garlic, minced
½ lb. smoked ham, cut up in
   1-inch pieces

1 tablespoon salt
2 teaspoons black pepper
1 cup red wine
3 whole **chorizos** (*Spanish*
   sausages)
4 tablespoons paprika
3 cups beef broth
¼ cup olive oil

Pierce a hole (about 1 inch in diameter) through the length of the *boliche*. Stuff with Spanish sausage and ham. Heat oil in a Dutch oven. Mix salt, pepper, oregano, and paprika and rub on outside of roast until it is well covered. Add onions, green pepper, and garlic. Brown *boliche* in Dutch oven. Add broth, red wine, and bay leaves. Cover. Cook over medium-low heat for approximately 2½ hours, turning several times. When done, remove from Dutch oven and process gravy in food processor until smooth. Cut *boliche* into ½-inch slices and pour gravy over it. Serve with white rice, black beans, and fried ripe plantains. Serves 8.

Filet Steak Columbia

Filete Bistec Columbia

1 6-oz. filet steak
2 strips bacon
½ green pepper, chopped
½ onion, chopped
¼ cup tomato sauce
2 tablespoons olive oil
1 teaspoon flour

Salt and pepper to taste
½ cup broth made with bouillon
  cube, or ½ cup brown sauce
  (see p. 201)
¼ cup red wine
4 mushrooms, sliced
1 teaspoon Worcestershire sauce

Salt and pepper steak and wrap in bacon strips. Sauté onion and green pepper with tomato sauce in oil for 10 minutes. Add flour and broth. Add wine, mushrooms, and Worcestershire sauce. Pan-broil steak and place in casserole. Pour sauce over it and bake at 450° for 2 minutes. Serves 1.

Filet Steak Milanesa

Filete à la Milanesa

2 6-oz. filet steaks
1 egg, slightly beaten
2 cups bread crumbs
Garlic powder, salt, and pepper
  to taste

¼ cup oil
2 cups Catalana sauce
  (see p. 201)
1 hard-boiled egg, chopped
Chopped parsley

Season steaks with salt, pepper, and garlic powder. Dip in beaten egg, then bread crumbs. Pan-fry in oil and transfer to an ovenproof plate. Spread Catalana sauce on top of steak. Bake at 400° for 5 minutes. Garnish with chopped egg and parsley. Serves 2.

Filet Steak Sauté

Filete Salteado

1 lb. tenderloin filet, cut in 1-inch
   cubes
1 Spanish onion, chopped
2 garlic cloves, chopped
¼ cup extra-virgin olive oil
1 **chorizo** (Spanish sausage), sliced
½ cup sliced mushrooms

Salt and pepper to taste
2 potatoes, peeled and diced
Vegetable or peanut oil for frying
⅓ cup red wine
1 green pepper, chopped
Green peas (cooked) and chopped
   parsley for garnish

Sauté diced tenderloin in hot olive oil. When meat is brown, add
chopped garlic, onion, and green pepper. Set aside. Deep-fry diced potatoes in vegetable oil for 10 minutes or until brown; drain on paper towels.
Add *chorizo*, mushrooms, salt, pepper, and potatoes to the meat. Add
wine and bring to a boil. Garnish with peas and parsley. Serves 2.

Filet of Tenderloin Capuchina

Filete Capuchina

9-oz. tenderloin steak
½ stick butter
½ Spanish onion, chopped
4 chicken livers, chopped
10 mushrooms, sliced

½ teaspoon salt
½ cup red wine
⅓ cup parsley, chopped
6 slivered almonds, toasted

Grill steak as desired. Prepare sauce by simmering butter with onion
and chopped livers. When onions are transparent, add salt, red wine, and

mushrooms. On a large piece of aluminum foil or parchment paper, place half the chicken liver sauce, then the steak, then the remainder of the chicken liver sauce, then the almonds and parsley. Close paper over top and fold edges together to seal. Bake at 500° for 3 minutes. Serve hot. Serves 1.

Filet of Tenderloin Steak Creole à la Ferdie Pacheco

Filete Criollo à la Ferdie Pacheco

2 6-oz. filets of tenderloin
1 cup canned whole tomatoes, chopped
½ cup olive oil
1 onion, chopped
1 sweet potato, peeled and sliced in ¼-inch rounds
2 white potatoes, peeled and sliced in ¼-inch rounds

2 medium-ripe plantains, peeled and sliced in ½-inch rounds
Salt to taste
1 cup red wine
2 cloves garlic, minced
1 green pepper, chopped
Vegetable or peanut oil for frying potatoes

Broil steak as desired and place in casserole. Heat olive oil in saucepan. Sauté onions, green peppers, and garlic until tender. Add tomatoes, salt, and red wine.

In another pan, fry sweet potatoes, plantains, and potatoes in vegetable oil until done. Add to sauce and cook for five minutes. Add sauce to steak in casserole. Bake for 10 minutes at 350°. Serve hot. Serves 2.

Fresh Pork Ham

Pernil de Puerco

1 fresh pork ham (about 6 lbs.)
1 cup sour orange juice
   (if not available, ½ cup lemon
   juice and ½ cup orange juice
   may be used)

8 large garlic cloves
2 teaspoons oregano
¼ teaspoon pepper
4 bay leaves
Salt to taste

Wash ham; pat dry. With a sharp knife, puncture ham in several places. Place in shallow roasting pan. Pour orange juice all over ham, then rub salt on it. Mash garlic, oregano, and pepper into smooth paste and rub on ham, pushing mixture into punctured holes. Add bay leaves to juice. Marinate for 6 to 8 hours or overnight. Roast at 350°, skin side up, for 3 hours. (For ham that weighs about 6 lbs., allow 30 minutes per pound; for hams that weigh 10 or more lbs., allow 20 minutes per pound.) Let ham stand at room temperature 30 minutes before carving. Serves 8.

Lamb Stew

Chilindrón de Cordero

2½ lbs. boneless lamb, cut into
   1½-inch cubes
4 tablespoons olive oil
¼ lb. salt pork, chopped
2 large Spanish onions, chopped
1 teaspoon chopped garlic
1 8-oz. can tomato sauce

½ teaspoon paprika
1 tablespoon chopped parsley
1 bay leaf
Salt and pepper to taste
Flour
½ cup dry sherry

Heat oil in deep skillet and fry salt pork. Dredge lamb in flour and brown in same oil. Set aside, discarding salt pork. Sauté onions in same oil until limp, adding more oil if needed. Add garlic and rest of ingredients. Return lamb to skillet and add salt and pepper. Cover and cook until meat is tender, about 1½ hours. Add wine when meat is tender and ready to be served. Serves 8.

Meatballs

Albóndigas de Carne

1 lb. ground beef
2 eggs
¾ cup bread crumbs
½ cup grated Romano cheese
½ cup water
1 teaspoon finely minced garlic

½ teaspoon oregano
½ cup olive or vegetable oil
Salt and pepper to taste
Tomato sauce (see spaghetti
    sauce # 2, p. 204)

Beat eggs with cheese, garlic, bread crumbs, oregano, and water. Add meat, salt, and pepper. Mix well. Form into balls (about the size of a golf ball). Brown lightly in oil. Drain. Cook for 20 minutes in tomato sauce. Makes 10 to 12 meatballs.

Pork Tenderloins

Filetes de Puerco

2 pork tenderloins, ¾ to 1 lb. each
6 garlic cloves, crushed
½ teaspoon oregano
Juice of 2 lemons

1 bay leaf
Salt and pepper to taste
Peanut oil

Marinate tenderloins overnight in mixture of garlic, oregano, bay leaf, and lemon juice. Salt and pepper tenderloins; brown in peanut oil in a skillet. Place in a baking dish. Pour remaining marinade over meat. Roast tenderloin ½ hour at 400°. Serves 8.

Shredded Beef

Ropa Vieja

1 flank steak (about 1½ lbs.), cut in 4-inch by 1-inch pieces	4 cloves garlic
	2 tomatoes, peeled and seeded
2 onions, chopped	1 bay leaf
1 green pepper, cut in strips	Salt to taste

Boil meat with other ingredients until meat is tender, approximately 1½ hours. Strain. When meat is cool, shred it as finely as possible. Puree vegetables in food processor.

SAUCE

2 large onions, sliced in half-moons	Salt and pepper to taste
1 large green pepper, cut in strips	1 15-oz. can tomato sauce
4 garlic cloves, minced	1 teaspoon oregano
1 bay leaf	Green peas (cooked) and pimento
½ teaspoon ground cumin	or roasted red pepper strips
2 tablespoons olive oil	for garnish
¼ cup red wine	

Sauté onions and green pepper in oil until tender. Add rest of ingredients and cook for 10 minutes. Add shredded beef and pureed vegetables. Stir well, cover, and cook for 30 minutes over medium-low heat. Garnish with green peas and pimento strips. Serve with white rice. Fried ripe plantains go very well with this dish. Serves 6.

Fish and Seafood

Pescados y Mariscos

Baked Whole Snapper

❧

Pargo Asado

1 5- to 6-lb. red snapper, dressed
   and scaled
8 garlic cloves, mashed
3 onions, thinly sliced
1 teaspoon oregano
Juice of 3 lemons

3 potatoes, peeled
3 tomatoes, sliced
1 cup extra-virgin olive oil
¼ teaspoon black pepper
Parsley for garnish
Salt to taste

Wash snapper inside and out. Pat dry and make two diagonal slits on each side. Make a paste of garlic, oregano, and pepper. (A mortar with pestle comes in handy for this; it may also be done with a small food processor.) Place snapper in a long shallow roasting pan. Drench with lemon juice inside and out. Salt to taste. Rub with garlic mixture, pushing some into slits. Refrigerate for 2 hours.

Just before baking fish, parboil potatoes, remove, and cut into ½-inch rounds. Remove fish from pan. Pour ½ cup olive oil evenly over bottom of pan, then layer sliced potatoes, onions, and tomatoes. Lay snapper on vegetables. Drizzle ½ cup of olive oil on fish and bake at 350° for 1 hour and 15 minutes. Decorate with parsley. This recipe works well for any whole whitefish. Serves 6.

Columbia Shrimp Supreme

Camarones Supremos de Columbia

16 jumbo shrimps, peeled
and deveined (tails on)
Juice of 1 lemon
1 teaspoon garlic powder
½ teaspoon pepper
1 teaspoon salt

8 thin strips bacon, cut in half
2 eggs, lightly beaten
½ cup milk
Flour
Vegetable or peanut oil for
frying

Pat shrimp dry and marinate in lemon juice, garlic, salt, and pepper for 10 minutes. Wrap half a strip of bacon around each shrimp and secure with toothpick. Beat together eggs and milk; dip each shrimp in batter. Roll in flour. Deep-fry at 300° until brown (about 5 to 8 minutes). Serves 2.

Fish Basque Style

Pescado à la Vasca

1 lb. grouper or red snapper fillets
1 large onion, cut in half-moon
slices
1 large green pepper, cut in strips
1 teaspoon chopped garlic
1 bay leaf
½ teaspoon oregano

½ cup olive oil
2 potatoes, boiled, peeled, and
cut in ½-inch slices
1 15-oz. can tomato sauce
1 tablespoon white wine
vinegar
Salt and pepper to taste

Sauté onion, green pepper, and garlic in olive oil. Add bay leaf, oregano, tomato sauce, salt, and pepper. Add fish fillets to sauce and poach for 7 minutes. Add vinegar, then potatoes, to sauce; simmer for 2 minutes. This is also delicious when made with white solid-packed canned tuna instead of fresh fish. Serves 2.

Fish in Green Sauce

Pescado en Salsa Verde

1½ lbs. whitefish fillets	*1 teaspoon salt*
6 cloves garlic	*¼ teaspoon white pepper*
½ cup extra-virgin olive oil	*2 tablespoons white vinegar*
4 Spanish onion rings	*½ cup dry sherry*
1 cup parsley	

Combine ingredients, except fish, in blender or food processor. Place fish fillets in skillet and cover with sauce. Cover and cook for 15 minutes. Serves 6.

Grouper à la Adela

Cherna à la Adela

2 grouper fillets	*1 cup Catalana sauce (see p. 201)*
1 egg, beaten lightly	*4 slices Swiss cheese*
1 cup seasoned bread crumbs	*2 tablespoons grated Romano cheese*
Garlic powder	*2 tablespoons extra-virgin olive oil*
Lemon juice	*Salt and pepper to taste*

Season fish fillets with lemon juice, garlic powder, salt, and pepper. Dip fish in egg; coat with bread crumbs. Heat oil in skillet over medium heat. Brown fillets lightly on each side. Transfer to shallow baking dish. Cover with Catalana sauce. Place 2 slices of Swiss cheese over each fillet and sprinkle with Romano cheese. Bake at 400° until cheese melts. Serve at once. Serves 2.

Grouper à la Rusa

Cherna à la Rusa

2 6-oz. grouper (or snapper)
   fillets
1 cup bread crumbs
1 cup flour
2 eggs, beaten lightly
⅓ cup chopped parsley

1 hard-boiled egg, chopped
Garlic powder
1 stick butter
1 lemon, thinly sliced
Salt and pepper to taste

Season fish fillets with garlic powder, salt, and pepper. Coat with flour. Dip in beaten eggs and coat with bread crumbs. Melt ½ stick of butter in heavy skillet over medium heat. When bubbly, pan-broil fillets until golden brown. Remove to platter. Melt remaining butter and pour over fillets. Arrange 3 or 4 slices of lemon on each fillet and garnish with chopped egg and parsley. Serves 2.

Lobster Cognac

Langosta Coñac

6 *steamed lobster or crawfish tails*
1 *tablespoon white pepper*
2 *sticks butter, melted*

1 *cup cognac (or other brandy)*
Pinch salt

Wash steamed lobster or crawfish tails and crack them; if they are large, cut them in half. Place in clay casserole and add salt, pepper, and butter. Bake at 450° for 10 minutes. Remove from oven, pour cognac over, and flame. Serve promptly. Serves 2.

Lobster Columbia

Langosta Columbia

½ *cup olive oil*
½ *medium onion, chopped*
½ *green pepper, cut in strips*
2 *garlic cloves, minced*
1 *tomato, peeled, seeded, and*
    chopped
¼ *cup smoked ham, chopped*

¼ *cup sliced mushrooms*
½ *lobster, shelled and cut in*
    1-inch pieces
5 *shrimps, peeled and deveined*
1 *cup chicken broth*
1 *cup white wine*

Heat olive oil in a deep frying pan. Add onion and green pepper and cook until wilted. Add tomato, garlic, mushrooms, ham, and broth. Add lobster and shrimp and cook over medium heat for 5 minutes. Remove from heat, add wine, and serve immediately. Serves 1.

Lobster Malagueña

―――――――――――― ❧ ――――――――――――

Langosta Malagueña

½ lobster tail, cut in 4 pieces
½ lb. smoked ham, cut in ¼-inch
    pieces
1 **chorizo** (Spanish sausage), cut
    in ¼-inch rounds
½ cup sliced mushrooms
½ green pepper, cut in strips
1 onion, chopped

2 cloves garlic, finely minced
¼ cup extra-virgin olive oil
1 8-oz. can tomato sauce
½ cup white wine
Salt and white pepper to taste
Asparagus spears and parsley
    for garnish

Heat olive oil in a deep skillet until a light haze forms above it. Sauté onion, green pepper, and garlic for 5 minutes; add tomato sauce. Add lobster and cook for 3 minutes over medium heat. Add ham, mushrooms, and *chorizo*. Stir well. Add half of wine. Cook 2 more minutes. Remove from stove and add rest of wine. Add salt and white pepper to taste. Garnish with 2 white asparagus spears and chopped parsley. Serves 1.

Operetta of Seafood

―――――――――――― ❧ ――――――――――――

Zarzuela de Mariscos

6 scallops
6 shrimps, peeled and deveined
1 cup coruñesa sauce (see p. 202)
¼ cup olive oil

2 tablespoons heavy cream
½ lobster tail, shelled and cut in
    4 pieces
2 tablespoons brandy

Heat oil in skillet and add seafood. Sauté 3 minutes. Add brandy and flambé. Add coruñesa sauce and simmer 1 minute. Add cream and simmer 1 more minute. Serve with rice or pasta. Serves 1.

Pompano Papillot

2 large or 4 small pompano steaks
¼ lb. butter
1 onion, finely chopped
1 cup flour
2 cups boiled milk
2 eggs
Dash Tabasco sauce

Dash nutmeg
2 tablespoons sauterne
½ lb. crawfish or lobster meat, chopped
½ lb. shrimps, peeled, deveined, and chopped

Sauté onion in melted butter for 5 minutes. Slowly add flour to form a roux. Let it cook dry, slowly. Add boiled milk and stir over medium heat to make thick cream sauce. Beat eggs with nutmeg, Tabasco sauce, and sauterne; fold into cream sauce. Add shrimp and crawfish or lobster.

On buttered parchment paper or aluminum foil (large enough to make a bag enclosing fish), spread ⅓ of the sauce and top with a slice of skinned pompano steak. Spread another ⅓ of the sauce, then another slice of pompano. Spread remaining sauce over top. Close paper or foil over top; seal by folding edges together. Brush melted butter over paper and bake 20 minutes at 400°. This dish may also be made with snapper or grouper. Serves 2.

Red Snapper Amandine

Pargo Almendrina

1 lb. red snapper fillets	*12 almonds*
½ cup drawn butter	*Juice of 1 lemon*
Salt and white pepper to taste	*3 dashes Worcestershire sauce*
½ cup flour	*Parsley leaves*

Salt and pepper snapper fillets; coat thoroughly with flour. Sauté in drawn butter. When brown, remove from saucepan and simmer almonds in same butter until brown. Add lemon juice and Worcestershire sauce. Garnish with parsley leaves. Serve immediately. Serves 2.

Red Snapper in Green Sauce

Pargo en Salsa Verde

4 red snapper fillets	*¼ cup white wine*
¼ cup extra-virgin olive oil	*½ cup clam juice*
1 tablespoon lemon juice	*Salt and pepper to taste*
1 teaspoon minced garlic	*½ cup minced parsley*
¼ cup minced onion	*Flour for coating fish*
2 tablespoons flour	*Chopped parsley for garnish*

Season fillets with salt and pepper; coat with flour. Heat half of oil in a large skillet. Brown fish on both sides and transfer to 4 individual oven-proof dishes. Sprinkle fish with lemon juice. Serves 4.

Wipe skillet, add remaining oil, and sauté onion and garlic until tender. Add 2 tablespoons flour, stir, and gradually add wine and clam juice. Stir over medium heat until sauce has thickened. Add parsley. Pour sauce over fish. Place dishes in oven at 400°. Bake about 15 minutes. Sprinkle with parsley before serving. Serves 4.

Red Snapper Fingers

Pargo Perlan

2 lbs. red snapper fillets	*2 eggs*
Juice of 1 lemon	*¼ cup olive oil*
Salt and white pepper to taste	*¼ cup peanut oil*
1 cup bread crumbs	

Cut fillets into 3- x 1-inch strips. Marinate in lemon juice, salt, and white pepper. Dip into beaten eggs and bread crumbs. Brown in skillet in mixture of olive oil and peanut oil. Drain, set aside, and keep warm.

SAUCE

3 tablespoons flour	*Salt and pepper to taste*
¼ cup butter	*1 hard-boiled egg, chopped*
1 cup milk	*Parsley, chopped*
1 cup sherry	

Heat butter in skillet. When melted, add flour. When flour turns light brown, add milk. Stir over medium heat until a light cream sauce forms. Add sherry, salt, and pepper. Pour over snapper fingers and garnish with chopped eggs and parsley. Serves 4.

Shellfish Vinaigrette

❧

Salpicón de Mariscos

1 lb. large shrimps (shells on)	1 bay leaf
1 lobster (shell on)	1 lemon slice
1 lb. cooked crabmeat (blue crab,	4 sprigs parsley
king crab, or stone crab),	2 slices onion
cartilage removed	2 garlic cloves, crushed
4 cups water	6 peppercorns
1 cup clam broth	

In a large pot simmer water, clam broth, bay leaf, lemon, parsley, onion, garlic, and peppercorns for 20 minutes. Add lobster and boil for 15 minutes. Remove lobster from liquid and cool. Add shrimp and boil for 4 minutes. Remove shrimp from liquid and cool. Peel shrimp and lobster; devein shrimp. Cut lobster into chunks. Make sauce below; add shrimp, lobster, and crabmeat. Mix well and chill overnight. Salt and pepper to taste. Serves 4.

SAUCE

1 cup extra-virgin olive oil	¼ cup minced Spanish sweet
1 cup white wine vinegar	onions
¼ cup capers	Salt and pepper to taste

Mix all ingredients in a glass or china bowl.

Shrimp Columbia

Camarones Columbia

1 large onion, chopped
1 green pepper, chopped
3 cloves garlic, chopped
¾ cup olive oil
1 8-oz. can tomato sauce, or
   1 cup canned whole tomatoes
1 bay leaf

32 medium shrimps, peeled
   and deveined
1 cup chicken consommé
20 small mushrooms
½ cup diced ham
½ cup red wine
1 teaspoon salt

Heat olive oil in skillet. Sauté green pepper, onion, and garlic over low heat. When tender, add tomato sauce or tomatoes, breaking them into small pieces. Add bay leaf, bring to a boil, and cook for 3 minutes. Add salt, mushrooms, ham, shrimp, and consommé. Cook for 5 minutes. Sprinkle with red wine and serve. Serves 4.

Shrimp Creole # 1 (with Tomato Sauce)

Camarones Criollo # 1 (con Salsa Tomate)

½ Spanish onion, chopped
½ green pepper, chopped
1 garlic clove, chopped
2 cups yellow or white rice,
   cooked
½ cup Spanish olive oil
½ cup tomato sauce

½ cup white wine
16 large shrimps, peeled and
   deveined
Salt to taste
Green peas (cooked) and pimento
   or roasted red pepper strips
   for garnish

Heat olive oil and add chopped garlic, green pepper, and onion. Sauté until onion is transparent. Add shrimp and cook over medium heat; when shrimp turns pink, add tomato sauce, white wine, and salt to taste. Put a cup mold of rice in middle of each plate; arrange shrimps around rice. Garnish with peas and pimento strips. Serves 2.

Shrimp Creole # 2 (without Tomato Sauce)

Camarones Criollo # 2 (sin Salsa Tomate)

*1 lb. large shrimps, peeled and
  deveined (tails left on)*
4 cloves garlic, minced
2 large onions, chopped
1 green pepper, cut in strips
1 bay leaf

2 teaspoons paprika
½ cup white wine or vermouth
8 sprigs parsley, chopped
½ cup olive oil
Salt and pepper to taste

Sauté onion and green pepper in olive oil until onion is transparent. Add garlic and bay leaf. Add shrimps; when they start turning pink, add paprika. Stir well and add wine, parsley, salt, and pepper. If sauce seems too thin, throw in a handful of bread crumbs (unseasoned). Serve with fluffy rice and fried ripe plantains. Serves 2.

Shrimp Kabobs Moorish Style

Camarones Moruno

3 lbs. large shrimps, peeled and
   deveined (tails left on)
1 cup olive oil
1½ teaspoons ground cumin
Juice of 1 lemon
3 teaspoons crushed red pepper
   (not cayenne)

1½ teaspoons paprika
3 bay leaves, crumbled
3 tablespoons minced parsley
3 garlic cloves, minced
½ cup dry white wine or sherry
Salt and pepper to taste

Mix all ingredients except shrimp in a food processor or blender. Combine with shrimp and stir to coat well. Cover and marinate in refrigerator for several hours or (for better flavor) overnight. Thread shrimps onto small skewers. Broil (or, better still, grill over coals) until light brown but still juicy (about 2 to 3 minutes). Baste with marinade. Serves 4.

Shrimp Sauté

Camarones Salteados

14 medium-size shrimps, peeled
   and deveined
2 tablespoons extra-virgin olive oil
⅓ cup Spanish onion, sliced
⅓ cup green pepper, cut in strips
⅓ cup dry white wine
½ **chorizo** (Spanish sausage),
   thinly sliced

½ teaspoon minced garlic
½ cup fresh sliced mushrooms
   (may also use canned)
1 small potato, peeled, cubed,
   and fried
⅓ cup brown sauce (see
   p. 201)

Heat oil in skillet. Sauté green pepper and onion until limp. Add garlic, *chorizo*, mushrooms, and fried potato. Cook over medium heat for 30 seconds. Add shrimp and cook 3 minutes. Add wine and brown sauce. Simmer for 2 minutes. Serves 1.

Shrimp Sautéed in Garlic

Camarones al Ajillo

¼ cup extra-virgin olive oil
6 garlic cloves, finely chopped
1 dried red chili pepper, cut in
    2 pieces, seeds removed
1 lb. medium shrimps, peeled and
    deveined

2 tablespoons chicken broth
3 tablespoons lemon juice
2 tablespoons chopped parsley
Salt to taste

Heat oil in a large skillet. Add garlic and chili pepper. When garlic just begins to turn golden, add shrimp and cook over high heat, stirring constantly. When shrimp turns pink, add broth and lemon juice. Season with salt and garnish with parsley. Serve immediately. Serves 2.

Shrimp in Tomato Sauce

❧

Camarones Enchilados

*1½ lbs. large shrimps, peeled and
deveined (tails removed)*
1 tablespoon olive oil

1 tablespoon minced garlic
1 red chili pepper, dried
2 cups enchilado sauce

Heat oil in skillet. Add shrimp, garlic, and chili pepper. Sauté for 2 minutes. Mix in 1 cup heated enchilado sauce. Serve with linguine or rice. Serves 4.

ENCHILADO SAUCE
1 cup white wine
2 green bell peppers, chopped
1 red bell pepper, chopped
2 onions, chopped
2 garlic cloves, chopped
½ cup chopped parsley
⅓ cup olive oil

1 teaspoon oregano
Pinch pepper
1 cup chicken stock
1 teaspoon Tabasco sauce
1 8-oz. can tomato sauce
Salt to taste

Sauté garlic and onions in olive oil until onions are transparent. Add peppers and parsley; continue to sauté. Add salt, pepper, oregano, tomato sauce, and chicken stock. Add wine and reduce by half. Add Tabasco sauce and bring entire mixture to a boil.

Snapper Alicante

— ❦ —

Pargo Alicante

1 lb. snapper fillets
1 onion, cut in round slices
2 green peppers, cut in rings
½ cup brown sauce (see p. 201)
¼ cup olive oil
12 almonds

½ cup white wine
½ teaspoon salt
Pinch white pepper
4 slices breaded eggplant
    (recipe below)
4 Shrimp Supreme (recipe below)

In a casserole (preferably clay), place fillets on top of onion slices. Spread olive oil, salt, white pepper, brown sauce, white wine, almonds, and green pepper rings over fish. Bake uncovered at 350° for 25 minutes. Garnish each serving with 2 shrimp supreme and 2 breaded eggplant slices. Serves 2.

SHRIMP SUPREME

4 large shrimps, peeled and
    deveined (tails left on)
Juice of half a lemon
½ teaspoon salt
¼ teaspoon pepper
½ teaspoon garlic powder

2 thin strips bacon, cut in half
1 egg, slightly beaten
¼ cup milk
Flour
Vegetable oil for frying

Marinate shrimp in lemon juice, salt, pepper, and garlic powder. Wrap half a strip of bacon around each shrimp and secure with a toothpick. Beat egg and milk together; dip shrimp in mixture, then roll in flour. Deep-fry until golden brown.

BREADED EGGPLANT

2 slices peeled eggplant, ½ inch
   wide
1 teaspoon salt

1 egg, slightly beaten
Bread crumbs
Vegetable oil for frying

Salt eggplant and drain on paper towels for half an hour. Rinse and pat dry. Dip each slice in egg, coat with bread crumbs, and deep-fry until golden brown.

Spanish Lobster

Langosta à la Catalana

½ cup extra-virgin Spanish olive oil
1 large onion, finely chopped
6 lobster tails, cut in 2-inch
   chunks (shells on)
6 garlic cloves, finely
   chopped
½ cup clam juice

⅓ cup brandy (preferably Spanish)
2 cups canned whole tomatoes,
   drained and finely chopped
Salt and pepper to taste
½ cup pimentos or roasted red
   peppers, finely chopped
½ cup white wine

In large saucepan, heat oil over low heat until a light haze forms over it. Sauté onion until transparent. Add garlic, tomatoes, pimentos, wine, and clam juice. Cook over medium heat, partially covered, about 10 minutes. Add lobster and cook about 5 minutes. Add brandy, salt, and pepper. Bring to a boil. Serve over white rice or pasta with crusty French or Cuban bread. Serves 4.

Stuffed Lobster

Langosta Rellena

2 lbs. lobster

1½ cups milk

1 cup flour

1 tablespoon olive oil

¼ cup butter

¼ cup Tabasco sauce

1 tablespoon salt

1 egg

¼ cup white wine

Remove meat from lobster and dice. Melt butter and oil in ovenproof skillet. Add flour, stirring until blended with butter and oil. Add milk, salt, Tabasco sauce, and egg. Stir until thick and smooth. Add wine and lobster. Dot with butter and bake at 400° for 10 minutes. Serves 2.

Ybor City Deviled Crab

Croquetas de Jaiba de Ybor City

CROQUETTE DOUGH

3 loaves stale American bread, sliced

1 loaf stale Cuban bread

1 level tablespoon paprika

1 teaspoon salt

Remove crust from American bread and discard. Soak remainder of bread in water for 15 minutes; drain and squeeze until almost dry. Grind Cuban bread very fine and sift. Add sifted Cuban bread to American bread gradually, mixing until dough is formed. Add paprika and salt. Mix thoroughly. Wrap and refrigerate for 2 hours.

CRABMEAT FILLING

5 tablespoons olive oil

3 onions, finely chopped

½ red or green bell pepper, finely
   chopped

4 garlic cloves, finely chopped

1 level teaspoon crushed red hot
   pepper (Italian style)

2 bay leaves

½ teaspoon sugar

1 level teaspoon salt

1 6-oz. can tomato paste

1 lb. fresh crabmeat (cartilage
   removed), shredded (claw meat
   is good for croquettes)

Sauté onions, bell pepper, garlic, and crushed pepper for 15 minutes over low heat. Add rest of ingredients and cook for 10 minutes covered. Remove bay leaves. Uncover and refrigerate.

ASSEMBLING CROQUETTES

2 eggs, well beaten

½ cup milk

Dash salt

Dash pepper

½ cup flour

1 cup dry bread crumbs

Vegetable or peanut oil for frying

Mix eggs, milk, salt, and pepper. Mix in bread crumbs and flour. Take about 3 tablespoons of croquette dough and press flat in your hand. Put in a tablespoon of crabmeat filling, fold over, and seal. Roll each croquette first in the bread crumb mixture, then in the egg mixture, and again in the bread crumb mixture. Refrigerate for 2 hours. Deep-fry in oil until light brown.

Chapter Six

Don Quixote Gets
Dressed Up

FERDIE: No sooner had Domenico Valenti's workers finished the elegant, one-of-a-kind dining room envisioned by Casimiro II, and Ivo de Minicis and Casimiro approved of the skillful workmanship, than fate took hold of the project.

The Spanish envoy, while visiting Tampa, dined in the new dining room one night and was enchanted by the beauty of the place. At the time Casimiro had not thought of an appropriate name for the room. The envoy remarked that he had just purchased a beautiful hand-painted tile of Don Quixote tilting with the windmills and did not know what to do with it. It had hung in the 1933 World's Fair Exposition in Chicago and won acclaim. He and Casimiro picked out a spot on the wall, and when the workmen had finished, it was evident that the piece dominated the room. It was just a step further to deduce that the room could only be called the Don Quixote Dining Room.

Not to be outdone by a Spaniard, a friend of Casimiro's who was in the Cuban Senate decided that the opposite corner now looked too bare. From Havana he sent a huge, elaborate, golden Moorish vase. Recognizing its value and beauty, Casimiro had Domenico Valenti build a pedestal and surround it with wrought iron to protect it.

Much of the tile seen throughout the Columbia was another example of Casimiro's serendipity. A good friend of his, an Italian named Mr. Muto, dealt in marble and tile and had come upon an extraordinary buy in Mexico.

La Fonda in 1943. The tile wainscoting depicts the Don Quixote story.
The picture above the wine rack is of General Douglas MacArthur.

Loving the Columbia and enjoying his friendship with Casimiro, he sold the entire shipment for around one hundred dollars. Twenty years later, in the fifties, it was appraised at sixteen thousand dollars, and in today's marketplace, it represents more money than it cost to build the Quixote.

One great feature of the restaurant is a set of three hundred tiles telling Cervantes' story of Don Quixote de la Mancha. The tiles are unique in that they are arranged in groups of three, so that the first tile tells the story in English, the next tile illustrates the story, and the next translates the same story

The Don Quixote bandstand, 1946. The Christmas tree was not one
of the year's decorating triumphs.

to Spanish. This presently forms the wainscoting of La Fonda, although many
other illustrated tiles can be found throughout the restaurant.

The finishing touches were added on the Quixote Room as need dictated.
Casimiro II foresaw the day when dining and dancing would be a feature,
when a top pianist would play, and, if his luck held up, his gifted daughter,
Adela, would play. For this, he built an elevated stage with a sound system.

ADELA: *How little I knew how much I would play on that stage. When I graduated from Juilliard my father did not want me on a concert tour. He wanted me
at home. So I stayed and played off and on for years, though I did some touring,
too. The strangest of these interludes occurred during the six-week waiters' strike
of 1949.*

*I was married and my son Casey was just a year old, but my father needed
me at the restaurant, so I reported for duty. I was shocked to find I was going to
play the piano **and** wait on tables.*

*Well, I'd never in my life carried a dish at the Columbia, but I sure learned
fast. One of my first customers asked me for a coffee **mitad y mitad,** half Cuban*

coffee and half boiled milk. For the life of me I couldn't figure out what he meant, so I deduced that he was asking for half Cuban coffee and half American coffee. Today, forty-three years later, I can still see the look of surprise and dismay on that poor man's face.

I was dressed as a male waiter, with black tie, waiter's jacket, tux pants, so it shocked the customers when I would jump onstage and play my set on the piano. One man told my father, "What a place you've got here; even waiters know how to play the piano."

All through the bitterness of that strike I was worried sick about my one-year-old son, who was in the hospital with acidosis and dehydration. In those days it was a life-and-death situation, so I would spend the nights at his side, run to the restaurant to work, come back to the hospital in the afternoons, and rush back at night to play and wait on tables.

All union disputes are terrible, and I thank God we've had very few in the ninety years we've been in business, but I still carry in my heart the pain of walking through a picket line of old and trusted employees. One particularly hurtful event stuck in my mind.

I was worried sick about Casey and exhausted from my schedule, and I had to walk through the picket line as I left to rush to the hospital. One of our most trusted waiters, a man who stayed with us for thirty-five years, confronted me and sarcastically said, "I guess you're good and tired now. That's how it feels to be a waiter."

Not a word about my child lying between life and death, not a conciliatory word, not a hope that this strike would be resolved soon, not a word of sympathy. This from a man I had known since I was a child. Oh, how it hurt. Even today I find it hard to be courteous to this man.

FERDIE: I loved to show people the wine cellar. No other restaurant had a subterranean, cool, dark place with racks of dusty bottles, and showing it off greatly enhanced my tip.

One day, a few years after the war, a young couple asked Pepin the headwaiter to see the wine cellar. When they were in the room they hesitantly asked Pepin if he would turn out the light and leave them alone. Pepin, being the ultimate romantic—also observing that the man was not carrying a corkscrew, and was a gentleman—obliged.

A few minutes later they emerged smiling. The young man had lipstick all over his face. "During the war I got shot down in France," he said. "A family hid me in a dark wine cellar for months. They had a daughter, and she would come down and keep me company in the dark." He looked lovingly at the beauty at his side. "So I married her, and we've been happy ever since, and now, on our anniversary, we lucked into your wine cellar, so we couldn't resist."

Pepin, with a twinkle in his eyes, sent over a bottle of the best wine.

No sooner was the Quixote Room finished and business booming than Casimiro began hatching up a new room.

Casimiro had had a slim education in Cuba, but he had developed a passion for knowledge. He read the encyclopedia from A to Z. He immersed himself in the classics of literature, and one of his passions was Spain, although he never set foot in the mother country.

In particular he soaked up photographs and descriptions of Sevilla and its architecture. Of all Spanish cities it most resembled Ybor City. Its people spoke in a slangy way, cutting off the last letters of a word, like the Cubans and Tampeños speak.

Once he made up his mind, and could envision what he wanted, he called his friend Ivo de Minicis to a work lunch. Ivo de Minicis was an Italian architect from Rimini. His knowledge of Italian and Spanish architecture was broad, and he was a cultured man. His main advantage was that he could translate into actuality what Casimiro could visualize in his brain.

This time Casimiro wanted an open Sevillano patio, surrounded by a balcony, with a big fountain in the middle and a wainscoting of decorative marble.

Working closely together, the team fashioned the bright, airy, happy Patio. Ivo sent away for a statue of a girl intertwined with a dolphin to go in the middle. The statue, which has become the most recognized symbol of the Columbia restaurants, is a terra-cotta replica of a sculpture found in the ruins of Pompeii and is believed to represent a mythical god of the ocean who fell in love with a sea nymph. It's called *Love and the Dolphin*.

The open roof presented problems that seemed insurmountable until Ivo

The Patio as seen from the Don Quixote doorway, 1946. The *Love and the Dolphin* statue is visible from the Don Quixote Room.

designed and installed a sliding glass roof. This Rube Goldberg invention proved erratic; rollers sometimes broke as the roof was cranked open, the glass panes cracked and broke with the heat, the load on the air conditioner was expensive, and so on. Eventually, years later, Casimiro decided to have it

The Patio entrance, showing beautiful wrought-iron work, 1947.

shut permanently, and an unbreakable glass skylight was installed. The Patio no longer affords open-air dining, but it does give the illusion of it.

An unexpected and unpleasant sequela of dining on the sunlit balcony was the unusual strain it put on the waiters. Not only were they half a block away from the kitchen but they also had to climb the stairs with each order. Waiters assigned there likened it to the Bataan Death March.

Casimiro's luck continued to hold up when he built the Patio. A Spanish captain, José Marín of Cádiz, brought his ship, the *Manolo Calvo*, to Tampa and dined in the Patio. He carried on his ship a collection of tiles illustrating the style of bullfighting favored by the famous Manolete. It became another welcome addition to the wall.

Today, lunch in the sunny, friendly Patio is the height of pleasant eating. Supper is also enchanting as night brings a different shading. The Patio, with its soft lighting, assumes a magical air, and romance is definitely in the air.

Beans and Rice Dishes

Arroz y Frijoles

Black Beans with Rice

Arroz con Frijoles Negros (Moros y Cristianos)

1 quart cooked black beans
  (see p. 34)
2 cups long-grain white rice,
  uncooked
4 cups water
1 large onion, chopped
1 large green pepper, cut in strips
1 teaspoon finely chopped garlic

2 bay leaves
1 teaspoon oregano
½ teaspoon ground cumin
¼ cup extra-virgin olive oil
Salt and pepper to taste
1 teaspoon hot sauce
1 tablespoon vinegar

In a large casserole, sauté onion and green pepper in olive oil. When onions are transparent, add garlic, oregano, bay leaves, salt, pepper, and cumin. Stir well. Add rice, water, black beans, hot sauce, and vinegar. Stir. Bring to a boil. Lower heat, cover, and cook for approximately 20 minutes. Test rice for doneness. Fluff rice with a large two-tined fork. Serves 6–8.

Brazilian Rice

Arroz Brazileño

4 cups cooked rice
3 carrots, diced
½ green pepper, diced
1 onion, diced
1 small can tiny green peas, or
  1 10-oz. package frozen peas

1 tomato, peeled, seeded and
  chopped
½ cup diced ham
1–2 tablespoons raisins (optional)
½ cup olive oil

Sauté vegetables and ham in oil until barely tender. (Do not brown.) Add rice and raisins; stir until thoroughly mixed. Serve piping hot. This is a good accompaniment for any meat or chicken dish. Serves 4.

Fried Rice Cuban-Chinese Style

Arroz Frito Estilo Cubano-Chino

3 cups cooked white rice (without salt)
1 lb. cooked pork, cut into small pieces
½ lb. smoked ham, cut in thin strips
½ lb. small shrimps, peeled, deveined, and boiled

3 tablespoons peanut oil
3 garlic cloves, mashed
¼ teaspoon fresh ginger, minced
6 eggs
4 tablespoons soy sauce
2 bunches scallions, chopped (green tops included)

Heat 1 tablespoon oil in large skillet. Beat eggs, pour into skillet, and make a very thin omelette. Cut omelette into strips like the ham. Set aside.

Heat rest of oil. Fry garlic until golden and discard. Add rice to oil and stir with a large two-tined fork until rice is well coated. Add pork, ginger, shrimp, ham, and egg. Stir well, add soy sauce, and stir in scallions. Serve immediately. Serves 4.

Good Rice

Arroz Bueno

1 stick butter
4 cups chicken broth (preferably
   homemade)
½ cup fresh basil, chopped
½ cup parsley, chopped

2 cups white long-grain rice,
   uncooked
1 large onion, chopped
Salt to taste

Melt butter and sauté onion until transparent. Add rice and stir constantly until it turns into a caramel color. Add chicken broth, then parsley, basil, and salt. Bring to a boil and lower flame. Cover and steam rice for 18 minutes. Fluff with a large two-tined fork. Serves 6 to 8.

Lima Beans Creole Style

Cacerola de Habas à la Criolla

1 lb. large lima beans, dried
6 cups water
½ lb. bacon, diced
1 onion, chopped
1 green pepper, diced
1 tablespoon flour

1 teaspoon salt
¼ teaspoon pepper
2 teaspoons prepared mustard
1 teaspoon Worcestershire sauce
2 tablespoons brown sugar
2½ cups tomato sauce

Rinse beans, cover with water, and boil for 2 minutes. Cover and let stand for 1 hour; cook over low heat until tender. Drain. Cook bacon in large skillet until crisp. Remove and drain bacon. Add onions and green pepper to bacon fat in skillet and cook for 5 minutes. Blend in flour, seasonings, and sugar. Add tomato sauce and simmer uncovered for 10 minutes. Add beans and heat. Sprinkle with bacon. Makes 6 to 8 servings.

Paella Havana

Paella Habana

½ cup white rice, uncooked
⅛ teaspoon yellow food coloring
¼ cup chopped onion
¼ cup chopped green pepper
1 teaspoon chopped garlic
⅓ cup boneless pork loin
⅓ cup cooked yucca
1 small sweet potato, peeled and
   cut in chunks
1 ripe plantain, peeled and sliced
   in 1-inch chunks

½ cup cooked black beans
¼ cup extra-virgin olive oil
2 tomatoes, peeled, seeded,
   and chopped
1 cup chicken broth
¼ cup white wine
1 teaspoon cooked green peas for
   garnish
Salt and pepper to taste

Heat oil in shallow (about 3 inches deep) ovenproof skillet or casserole. Sauté onions, green peppers, tomatoes, and garlic. Add pork loin and cook over low heat until tender; if needed, add a little broth. Add yucca, sweet potatoes, plantains, black beans, salt, and pepper. Add chicken broth, rice, and food coloring. Stir well and bake at 400° for 20 minutes. Sprinkle with wine and garnish with peas. Serves 1.

Paella Oriental

1 egg
2 tablespoons peanut oil
1 cup cooked white rice
¼ cup sliced fresh mushrooms
2 tablespoons chopped green onions
2 tablespoons chopped green pepper
2 tablespoons bean sprouts

⅓ cup cooked chicken breast,
    cut in strips
¼ cup cooked pork loin, cut in cubes
4 shrimps, peeled, deveined, and
    cooked
¼ cup snow peas
½ cup soy sauce

Heat 1 tablespoon oil, beat egg, and make a thin omelette. Set aside and cut into thin strips. Heat remaining oil in heavy skillet. Sauté rice lightly with mushrooms. Add remaining ingredients and egg strips. Heat thoroughly and serve at once. Serves 1.

Paella Valenciana

½ lb. pork, cut in chunks
1 onion, chopped
½ chicken (fryer), cut in 4 pieces
1 green pepper, chopped
1 lb. lobster, cut in chunks
3 garlic cloves, minced
½ lb. shrimps, peeled and deveined
1 bay leaf
8 oysters, shucked
½ cup whole tomatoes, chopped
8 scallops
½ cup olive oil
8 mussels (shells on)

1½ cups rice, uncooked
4 clams (shells on)
1 teaspoon salt
4 stone crabs or blue crabs (shells
    cracked)
Pinch saffron
1 lb. red snapper, cut in chunks
¼ cup white wine
3 cups fresh seafood or chicken stock
Small green peas (cooked), sliced
    pimentos or roasted red peppers,
    and asparagus spears for garnish

Pour oil in heavy, shallow casserole. Add onion and green pepper and sauté until limp but not brown. Add tomatoes, garlic, and bay leaf. Cook for 5 minutes. Add pork and chicken and sauté until tender, stirring to prevent sticking or burning.

Add seafood and stock. When this mixture boils, add rice, salt, and saffron. Stir. Bring to a boil, cover, and bake in oven at 350° for 20 minutes. When ready to serve, sprinkle with wine and garnish with peas, asparagus, and pimentos. Serves 4.

Red Beans Cuban Style

Potaje de Frijoles Colorados à la Cubana

⅓ cup extra-virgin olive oil
1 large Spanish onion, chopped
1 large green pepper, cut in strips
6 garlic cloves, minced
1 8-oz. can tomato sauce
2 bay leaves
1 teaspoon oregano
½ teaspoon cumin
3 29-oz. cans red kidney beans,
  including liquid

*2 **chorizos** (Spanish sausages),*
  cut in thin slices
½ lb. smoked ham, cut in 1-inch
  chunks
1 butternut squash or 1 lb. Cuban
  pumpkin, peeled and cut in
  2-inch chunks
2 medium-size potatoes, peeled
  and cut in 8 pieces each
Salt and pepper to taste

Heat olive oil in large soup kettle and sauté onion, green pepper, garlic, bay leaves, oregano, and cumin. When onions are transparent, add tomato sauce, *chorizos,* and ham. Stir. Add squash (or pumpkin) and potatoes. Cook for 5 minutes, then add beans. Add salt and pepper to taste. If mixture seems too thick or dry, add one cup of water or beef broth. Serves 6.

Red Beans with Rice

Congrí

1 quart cooked red beans	2 bay leaves
2 cups long-grain rice, uncooked	1 teaspoon oregano
4 cups water	½ teaspoon ground cumin
1 large Spanish onion, chopped	¼ cup extra-virgin olive oil
1 large green pepper, chopped	1 teaspoon hot sauce
1 teaspoon finely chopped garlic	Salt and pepper to taste

Sauté onion and green pepper in olive oil in a large casserole. Add garlic, oregano, bay leaves, and cumin. Stir well. Add rice, water, beans, salt, pepper, and hot sauce. Stir, bring to a boil, lower heat, cover, and cook for 20 minutes. Serves 6.

Rice with Corn

Arroz con Maíz

8 slices bacon	2 cups long-grain rice, uncooked
1 large onion, chopped	4 cups liquid (combine liquid from
2 15-oz. cans whole kernel corn,	canned corn and water)
drained (may also use 4 cups	2 teaspoons salt
fresh corn, scraped from cob)	

Fry bacon until crisp. Drain and set aside. Sauté chopped onion in bacon grease. When onion is transparent, add corn, rice, liquid, and salt. Stir well, cover, and cook over low heat for 20 minutes. When ready to serve, garnish with crumbled bacon. This is a great side dish to serve with breaded steaks or barbecued chicken or ribs. Serves 6.

Rice and Squids

Arroz con Calamares

⅓ cup Spanish olive oil
2 cups water
1 medium onion, chopped
1 cup rice, uncooked
1 green pepper, cut in strips
2 cans Spanish squid
2 cloves garlic, finely chopped

¼ cup white wine
Salt and white pepper to taste
2 bay leaves
Green peas (cooked) and pimento
 or roasted red pepper strips for
 garnish

Heat olive oil in ovenproof skillet or casserole. Sauté onion, green pepper, and garlic until limp. Add bay leaves and squid. Add rice and water. Salt and pepper to taste. When water boils, stir well, cover, and bake in oven for 20 minutes at 400°. Before serving, sprinkle with wine and garnish with peas and pimentos. Serves 2.

Seafood Rice Columbia

Arroz Marinera Columbia

½ cup Spanish olive oil
1 green pepper, chopped
¼ lb. snapper fillet, cut in chunks
2 cloves garlic, minced
8 jumbo shrimps, peeled and
 deveined
1 cup white wine
15 scallops

1 onion, chopped
1 teaspoon salt
2 cups seafood broth or water
1½ cups Valencia or long-grain rice,
 uncooked
Green peas (cooked) and pimento
 or roasted red pepper strips for
 garnish

Heat olive oil in ovenproof skillet or casserole. Add shrimp, snapper, and scallops; cook over medium heat until shrimp turns pink. Add garlic, green pepper, and onion and sauté until limp. Add seafood broth, white wine, and salt. As mixture starts to boil, add rice, cover, and bake at 350° for 15 minutes. Garnish with peas and pimentos. Serves 2.

Spanish Yellow Rice

Arroz Amarillo

½ cup extra-virgin olive oil
1 large Spanish onion, chopped
1 medium-size green pepper, cut
   in strips
4 garlic cloves, minced
2 bay leaves
2 tomatoes, seeded, peeled, and
   chopped

2 cups long-grain rice, uncooked
½ teaspoon saffron or yellow food
   coloring
2 teaspoons salt
4 cups chicken broth
Green peas (cooked), pimento or
   roasted red pepper strips, and
   parsley for garnish

In casserole or ovenproof skillet, heat olive oil. Sauté onion, green pepper, garlic, tomatoes, and bay leaves. Add rice, saffron, salt, and chicken broth. Bring to a boil, lower heat, cover, and cook for 18 minutes, either on top of stove (medium-low) or in oven (400°). Garnish with peas, pimentos, and parsley. This is a very good side dish for fish, chicken, or meat. Serves 2 as main dish.

Yellow Rice with Shrimps

❦

Arroz Amarillo con Camarones

½ cup extra-virgin olive oil
1 lb. large shrimps
1 large Spanish onion, chopped
1 large green pepper, cut in strips
4 cloves garlic, finely minced
3 cups shrimp broth
2 tomatoes, peeled, seeded, and
   chopped
1½ cups long-grain rice, uncooked
¼ cup white wine

2 teaspoons white wine vinegar
2 bay leaves
1 teaspoon salt
1 teaspoon hot sauce
Pinch saffron or ½ teaspoon yellow
   food coloring
Green peas (cooked), pimento or
   roasted red pepper strips, and
   parsley leaves for garnish

Peel and devein shrimp, saving shells for broth. (Boil shells in 3½ cups of water, covered, for 20 minutes; strain.) Heat olive oil in heavy casserole and sauté onion and green pepper until limp. Add garlic and tomatoes. Cook 2 minutes over medium heat. Add shrimp, bay leaves, wine, vinegar, and hot sauce. Add hot broth, saffron, and salt. When broth comes to a boil, add rice, cover, and bake in oven at 400° for 20 minutes or until rice is done. Garnish with peas, pimento strips, and parsley leaves. Serves 2.

White Rice

Arroz Blanco

2 cups long-grain white rice,
    uncooked
4 cups water
2 garlic cloves, mashed

2 teaspoons salt
2 tablespoons peanut oil
1 teaspoon lemon juice

Heat oil in a shallow saucepan (about 3 inches deep and 10 inches in diameter). Fry garlic in hot oil until golden, being careful not to burn. Discard garlic. Coat rice with oil. Add water, salt, and lemon juice. Bring to a boil, lower heat, cover, and steam for 18 minutes. Fluff the rice with a large two-tined fork and serve. Serves 6.

Chapter Seven

WHEN THE
VIOLIN CHASED
THE PIANO

FERDIE: Adela Hernandez at fifteen years of age was a pert, cute teenager with a beautiful smile and a warm personality. Her strict upbringing could not stifle a glowing spirit, and she was well liked and courted by her classmates. Although it represented a great advantage to be known as Casimiro's daughter, Adela did not advertise the fact that her family owned the Columbia. She didn't hide it, nor did she volunteer the information. She was mostly seen as a good student who was a child prodigy at the piano.

Cesar Gonzalez Martinez (later combined as Gonzmart) was a tall, handsome boy who had a flair for dressing well. Then, as later, he seemed years older than his actual age of fifteen and was a master salesman who bent the truth to his purpose when it suited him. He was very popular and was looked up to as a gifted violinist. He did not fail to make it known that he was the first violinist in the Columbia Restaurant orchestra.

When Cesar set his sights on the pert Adela, he did not know that she was in any way connected to the Columbia Restaurant. He met her when they both were assigned to perform with the Tampa WPA Symphony. Adela was to solo in a Grieg piano concerto; Cesar would lead the violin section. The problem was that the rehearsals were at the Tampa Auditorium, behind the University of Tampa, and Adela had no way to make it across town from Hills-

Mother Carmen, Baby Adela, 1½ years old, and Father Casimiro II, 1921.

borough High School. This provided Cesar with his opening, for he was the proud owner of a vintage Plymouth coupe. Adela accepted the rides and said nothing to her parents.

The relationship was platonic until Adela reached her sixteenth birthday, at which time Cesar invited her to catch an early movie at the Park Theater, across the street from the university. Adela's luck never ran well when it came

Adela, a four-year-old Marie Antoinette who said, "Let them eat Cuban bread."

to pulling a fast one on Casimiro. Just as they were buying the tickets, her Uncle Lawrence happened by and spotted them. He promptly told Casimiro that he had seen Adela at the movies with a boy. Because she had not asked permission, Adela's father was much displeased, but she was allowed out of the doghouse to go to the Columbia for her birthday supper.

Cesar had been bragging to Adela about the important role he played in the Columbia orchestra and, moreover, had promised her that if she came to dine at the restaurant he would introduce her to the owner.

Adela sat with her mother and aunt, enjoying the rare evening in the Quixote Room, when Cesar, finishing a set, spotted her. Delighted that she had come to see him play, he glided over to meet Adela and her family. Maintaining a straight face, Adela introduced her family. Casimiro, seeing the tall, handsome violinist talking to his family, came over hurriedly.

"And this is my father," Adela said, flashing her most beautiful smile. This marked the end of the first of Cesar's many attempts to court Adela. He not only lost the girl, he lost his job as well. When he discovered that this was the fellow Adela had met at the movies without his permission, Casimiro fired him on the spot.

Bloodied but unbowed, Cesar, who had worked hard to graduate from Hillsborough High at the age of fifteen, got on his motorcycle and drove to Stetson University and enrolled in the music department. He remained there for two years. Adela, in the meantime, graduated and started to look for a top school up north.

Her primary choices were the Curtis Institute of Music in Philadelphia and the famous Juilliard School of Music in New York. With her suitcases and parents, Adela took a train to Philadelphia, took a look at Curtis, and promptly

Adela, age six, at her first piano recital (second row, far right). Her teacher (center) was Pennsylvania Pacheco, Ferdie's step-grandmother.

turned it down. The family hated the city. They went on to New York to see if they could find a top teacher to prepare Adela for the hard-to-get-into Juilliard.

I am a firm believer in serendipity, or luck, or fate. Now came a moment of sheer serendipity.

One of Casimiro's old customers and suppliers of meat was a butcher named Mario Rodriguez who had migrated to New York City when things got too tough in Tampa. Casimiro decided to give him a call, just to touch base. Happy to hear from Casimiro, the butcher invited the family to go out to supper.

During the meal Adela told him that she was in New York to study piano. He mentioned that he delivered meat regularly to a Spanish concert pianist named José Itiburri. Adela put two and two together and came up with Iturbi: José Iturbi, the most popular concert pianist of the late 1930s. Would he ask Iturbi to hear Adelita play?

"Of course. I'll call him right now."

They held their breath as he plopped a dime in the pay phone and spoke for a minute or two. He returned to the table beaming. "He says to come on up. He's doing nothing right now!"

They took a cab to Eighty-third and Riverside Drive and dashed to Iturbi's lavish apartment. There they were met by José and his even more accomplished sister, Amparo. Adela played, and they accepted her immediately as a private student. The Iturbis played the piano in a style that was unique to them. Instead of playing with fingers extended and supple, they made trip-hammers of their fingers, banging the keys and obtaining a unique sound while demolishing the keyboard.

For three years Adela lived in a dream world, studying with the Iturbis and accompanying Francescatti, the great violinist, and Giovanni Martinelli, the popular operatic tenor, in concerts and meeting the friends of José and Amparo Iturbi at their many private parties.

During these invaluable three years of hard work, Adela put her social life on hold. Her redoubtable mother and keeper, Carmita, lived with Adela and accompanied her everywhere she went. Casimiro, the consummate family man, came up once a month on the train. It took twenty-four hours to get

Adela, the most promising concert pianist produced by Ybor City, at her piano at age fifteen.

from Tampa to New York. It must have been a tough three years for Casimiro.

About this time, when Adela was preparing for her entrance audition at Juilliard, her mother decided to take her to the 1939 World's Fair in Flushing Meadow, the event of the decade. Adela visited the Florida Pavilion and was amazed to find the tall, good-looking violinist Cesar selling ice cream cones at the counter. Laughing at the embarrassed Cesar caught in a menial task, Adela asked what had happened to him. When she had last seen him, he was perfectly groomed and dressed in spotless and impeccably correct clothes. Now his hair was long and shaggy and his collar tips almost reached the top of his zoot pants, which were held up by wide suspenders and a pencil-thin belt, buckled at the side. The pants ballooned out at the knees and came to a point in very narrow cuffs. Adela and Carmita were shocked. Was this what had become of Cesar?

Ever the quick mouth, Cesar loaded up two cones of tangerine ice cream, handed them to the two startled ladies, no charge, of course, and started in on a fanciful explanation. This was an interim job he had taken to help out a friend; he was actually in New York to audition for the NBC Symphony, or the Met, and so on. Poor Cesar, for once caught without his violin, and his "front"!

He begged Adela for a date. Under the stern eye of her mother, she told the pleading Cesar to come see her at their apartment. Knowing that she was going to move, she gave him the old address. Cesar could not contain his happiness, although he wondered why her mother hadn't protested.

They were moving because Carmita had found out that the German-American couple who owned the building and lived on the ground floor were having meetings of the German-American Bund, a Nazi organization, and she felt threatened there. They moved to another apartment closer to Juilliard. Adela told the owner if a certain tall gentleman came to call not to give him her new address. Imagine poor Cesar's devastation when he knocked on the door and was met by a "Sieg Heil" and a stiff salute.

Having passed her entrance audition at Juilliard, Adela looked at the list of teachers and found the best to be Carl Friedberg. Being full of the confidence of youth and having studied for three years with the Iturbis, she felt ready. She asked for and got an appointment with Mr. Friedberg, a tough old drillmaster who had the distinction of being the last living pupil of Clara Schumann, the wife of composer Robert Schumann. Her unstable husband had gone to a surgeon to have an operation that would give him a wider finger spread. Surgery being what it was at the end of the century, it is no surprise to report a failure so complete that Robert Schumann could no longer play the piano, and Clara had to play all his compositions for him. Such is the tale Carl Friedberg told.

Adela sat at the piano in a drab room. Mr. Friedberg eyed her coldly. He was a little old man, bent over from arthritis, with wiry wisps of hair covering his head. The only sound heard was his asthmatic breathing.

"Whatever gives you the idea that you can play good enough to be entitled to be taught by me?"

Adela was struck dumb. She looked at her hands, took a breath, and, with her head down, mumbled, "Let me play for you. You will see."

The old man harrumphed. She felt she might be gaining ground.

"You've been studying here for three years, with whom?"

Cesar at fifteen, the first violinist of the Don Quixote orchestra.

"José and Amparo Iturbi."

"Ach, the bent-finger people!" The old man stood up and held out his gnarled fingers in an arthritic imitation of the famous Iturbi position.

"I played normally, before they changed me, and I can play that way again." Adela was getting a little confidence and had a little fire in her voice. The old man liked that.

"What have you chosen to play?"

Relieved, Adela blurted out, "A Mozart sonata, a Chopin ballade in G minor, and 'Cordoba' by Albeniz."

He said, "Begin, please."

When it was over he told her that she had talent and he would take her as his pupil. He insisted that she take a full college curriculum.

Carl Friedberg took only five students at a time, and in Adela's class, two became famous, Ferrante and Teischer.

A D E L A : *I studied hard at Juilliard for four years, but the time passed quickly. I found myself in a heady environment, surrounded by brilliant teachers and talented students anxious to learn. It was more than I had imagined it could be.*

As the graduation exam approached I began to get unreasonably nervous. All of the years of hard study would come to one test, one graduation exam. It wasn't really an exam. It was more like an audition, or a one-woman mini-concert.

I walked to school as I had every morning, but this day was different. I was trembling as I walked. The exam was one of the most terrifying events of my entire life.

I had never had a psychic phenomenon happen to me or to anyone in my family, so I wasn't prepared for what happened next.

I was ready to begin playing, but I was so nervous I froze. Then, standing in front of me, facing me, was the figure of my grandfather, Viejo. He was dressed exactly as the last time I had seen him. He had a kind and serene look on his face.

Suddenly, I felt safe and secure, and the terror left me. Then I heard his voice clearly.

"It's going to be all right, Adelita. You're going to be fine."

He disappeared when I hit the first note, and he has never appeared to me again to this day. I don't know what to believe about psychic phenomena, but I can attest to this one example. Viejo was there when I needed him most. I passed my exam and graduated from Juilliard in 1944.

F E R D I E : The sun was setting over Tampa Bay, and we had been working on these stories since eight in the morning. Adela had been feeling poorly because arthritis had attacked her right hand, and she was in pain. At this point she looked up from the crates of photographs, letters, menus, and recipes we had spread across the room.

"Here's my Juilliard diploma," she smiled. "I almost lost it. I had it rolled up for twenty-five years, and when we moved to this house from across the street we had a bunch of friends and kids help us move all those boxes. When we were through, someone said, 'There is a rolled-up piece of paper rolling over the grass.' We were all so tired that nobody was curious enough to find out what it was except one of my boys, who ran to get it before it disappeared down the street. And guess what? It was my Juilliard diploma. Cesar said, 'Adela, you must get that framed.' So here it is."

My wife, Luisita, and I sat spellbound through the story of the exam, and I asked her to hum a few bars of "Cordoba." Luisita, who loves that piece, began to hum it. Adela immediately sprang from her chair, went to her grand piano, sat down, and began to play.

She became transformed. Her face, her body language, the expressive use of her arms and hands gave her the appearance of a young girl, playing her heart out for an adoring audience. The heavenly music flowed from the piano. We were stunned. I looked over and Luisita was crying as the splendid music struck her artist's heart.

The last note sounded softly. We applauded wildly, and before we could say anything, Adela spoke.

"That was Albeniz, but the 'Cordoba' by Ernesto Lecuona is better."

Again she played with warmth and feeling. She was right. Lecuona's piece had the fire and heart of the Caribbean to augment the sentiment of "Cordoba."

She had played without music, without practice, rehearsal, or warming up, and she had forgotten the pain of her arthritic right hand, proving once again that music has great therapeutic benefit.

My mind was racing ahead. How had a talent of this magnitude been immersed in the mundane life of being a housewife and mother? I knew the story ahead of us was the story of the romance of Adela and Cesar.

ADELA: *After I graduated I remained in New York for a while playing concerts, and since I was twenty-four years old by then, my mother no longer felt the need to watch over me. I was allowed to stay with a roommate and follow my career.*

Not that Daddy didn't keep his eye peeled, and, when it looked like I was getting serious with a boy, he would always take me to Cuba to cool off.

Succumbing to a siege of homesickness and missing the close companionship of my mother and father, I went back to Tampa. I met an Italian man from Ybor City and decided that I was in love. My father felt he was all wrong for me. He didn't dislike him; he actively hated him. That made me like him all the more. It's an old theme in literature and music, you know.

Casimiro II and Carmen in 1955, happily wed for thirty-six years.
This picture was taken at the fiftieth anniversary of the Columbia.
Notice that Casimiro was never short of pencils for signing tabs.

I was determined to marry this young man, so my mother and father re-lented. We had the invitations printed, and I went to Cuba with my mother to have my wedding dress made at the Parisian department in El Encanto, an ex-clusive store in Havana.

My father eventually softened and told me to invite my fiancé to a Father's Day brunch at our home. The brunch went well enough, and my father knocked himself out to make him feel at home, but he was suspicious and not too recep-tive. Finally, in a supreme effort to please, my daddy decided to partake of his favorite after-dinner drink with my fiancé. I was shocked, for he treasured every ounce of his hard-to-get elixir of Bacardi. I brought the bottle, which was in the shape of a globe with a long neck.

Proudly, my dad placed the bottle before my boyfriend, who promptly said, "That's what the low-class people drink."

The brunch ended abruptly. However, Daddy still seemed resigned to an in-evitable mistake.

The next day he asked me to grant him a wish: he wanted to take me and my mother to Cuba for a few days' vacation before my wedding. I agreed and said that would be fine. So I called my fiancé and told him that we would be gone for only a short while.

FERDIE: Serendipity now enters the picture again. Casimiro liked the white linen suits that tailors made so well in Havana, so one day while Adela and her mother were at the beach he strode into a tailor's shop only to find Cesar Gonzalez, being fitted for several suits. To his considerable surprise he found himself happy to see Cesar. As Casimiro listened to Cesar's fanciful story of how someone had stolen his suitcase full of clothes, suits, and tuxedos and how now, since he was a violinist in the Havana Symphony, he needed a new wardrobe, Cesar hatched a plot.

Cesar invited Casimiro to dine at the Zaragozana, one of the best restaurants in town. Casimiro, ever a man of honesty, told Cesar that Adela was to be married soon. Undaunted, Cesar insisted that this news was all the more reason to dine together.

ADELA: *Imagine my shock when I came back from the beach and found Dad beaming with joy, as if he had hit the bolita.*

"Guess who I just saw?"

"Who?" my mother and I asked in one voice.

"Cesar," beamed my father.

"Cesar who?" we asked.

"Cesar Gonzalez, the violinist."

"Oh, him," I said, disappointedly thinking of another Cesar I had liked. "The zoot suiter?"

"No, no," my dad was uncommonly excited. "You should see him now. He's at least an inch taller, slim, handsome, and he is doing very well. I saw him at the tailor's buying a whole new wardrobe. He's first violinist with the symphony."

My mother looked at me as if my dad had lost his mind.

"Well, hurry up, get dressed, we're going to meet him at the Zaragozana Restaurant. He's invited us to dinner."

Well, I thought, it's a way to spend a nice evening.

Cesar showed up with a corsage of gardenias for me and another for mom.

FERDIE: Gardenias.

ADELA *(making a face): I hate gardenias.*

FERDIE: Cesar pulled out all the stops and spent the meal romancing Adela's mother, who fell like a ton of bricks for his slick spiel. Cesar could bury you with charm. Few could resist him.

They ordered a paella; it was wonderful. When supper ended, Cesar signed a sizable tab with a flourish, getting the fish eye from the skeptical waiter in return.

ADELA *(laughing): This was before the days of credit cards.*

FERDIE: Then, with Casimiro's blessing, Cesar took Adela to El Zombie, the top Havana nightspot, for a nightcap and dancing. If there was ever a place to romance a girl out of the notion of getting married to somebody else, surely Havana of the 1940s was the place.

Undaunted by Adela's insistence that she was going to get married, Cesar continued to lay siege.

Finally the time came to return to Tampa and the husband-to-be. Remember serendipity? It's time for it to reappear.

Carmita had gone to say goodbye to some friends who lived in a mansion. As Casimiro and Adela were kissing their hosts, Carmita backed up and fell down a flight of marble stairs. With bruises, abrasions, contusions, and a fractured clavicle, she was too injured to move to the hospital, and the family insisted she and Adela stay at the mansion until she was healed.

The news energized the determined Cesar. Now he escalated the siege. Horse races, beach regattas, concerts, late nights at the Tropicana. Adela slowly crumbled. In the meantime her fiancé was calling every day to see when she would return to Tampa. The end came when he told Adela that she had been spotted by a friend of his at the Tropicana dancing with Cesar. Adela, worn out by the flattering assault of Cesar and having doubts about the impending wedding in the face of parental disapproval, had had enough. She told her fiancé, "The wedding is off."

ADELA: *Before I knew it, Cesar got wind of the breakup, and he was at my house with a six-and-a-half-carat emerald-cut diamond. I was in shock. I'd just gotten out of one engagement!*

"I can't accept that," I said. "I haven't even said yes."

Cesar had confidence and a winning way. "You will," he said, smiling his onstage smile. "You will."

A determined Cesar lays siege to Adela in Havana at the Zaragozana Restaurant, with the ever-present parents in attendance.

No sooner had I said yes than a bombshell exploded. Daddy came home with the shocking news that Cesar was married!

FERDIE: Nothing or no one could stop Cesar when he was on a roll and nearing the finish line.

Nimbly skipping over the fact that he was married, he informed Adela that he was organizing a concert for her in the prestigious Lyceo. He also explained that he was separated, and divorce proceedings were under way. Adela was mollified for the moment.

ADELA: *That Cesar could talk. At one point he tried to convince me that Walt Disney had named an entire feature film after his wife when he saw her dance. His wife's name was Fantasia. Even I had to laugh at that one.*

When things got quiet and I got used to the fact that he was married, he dropped the other shoe. He also had a son!

FERDIE: Worn out by the ups and downs of the romance, Adela agreed to get married in Tampa on December 27, 1946, much to the relief of her exhausted parents.

Imagine the face of the seamstress in Havana who had to design a new dress for Adela, who had just recently picked up her dress for a June wedding. Now she ordered another gown for a December wedding.

ADELA: *I didn't think it was right to get married in a dress I bought to marry another man and then wear it for my marriage to Cesar. I cut off the train and wore it in my personal appearances as a concert dress.*

FERDIE: But fate, which had been working overtime in Havana, was about to strike again in Tampa.

ADELA: *You can't imagine the planning it took to do this wedding. It was to be the wedding of the year. The guest list was huge. We reserved Sacred Heart Church downtown. The Columbia was going to close the Quixote and the Patio for the night. The presents filled our two-car garage and half the house. It was hectic. The day approached.*

On December 26, at eleven o'clock in the morning, the phone rang. It was Ferdie's father, J.B. He sounded very serious.

"Let me talk to Casimiro."

"He's asleep. He doesn't let me wake him up."

"Adelita, I'm telling you, wake him up."

Well, Ferdie's father was a close friend of Lawrence and my father, and when he said that, my heart stopped. I knew something horrible had happened.

And it had. My beloved Uncle Lawrence had dropped dead of a sudden overwhelming heart attack. He was forty-six years old.

What to do about the wedding?

FERDIE: The headline in the *Tampa Tribune* on the story said, "Death Cancels Wedding."

The house was in a turmoil. Adela immediately rushed to console Gloria, the widow. All the flowers ordered for the wedding were consigned to the funeral home. One of the biggest funerals Tampa had ever seen took place, and after the interment Gloria came to Adela and said, "I insist that you go through with your wedding."

What would have been a joyous and festive event turned into a small, serious affair. Only the immediate family went to the church. They dressed for the wedding, and while the photos don't reveal the ache in their hearts, they also don't reveal great joy. A very small party for family only was held in Casimiro's home.

The bride and groom, 1946.

And so, when the smoke cleared, Cesar had won the hand of Adela. The wedding was over, but the honeymoon lay ahead.

ADELA: *Dad had given me a brand new Buick, and we agreed to drive it to Washington, D.C., and New York, where I had several concert dates to fulfill. We bundled up against the cold and headed north, putting all the grief and tragedy behind us.*

But problems caught up with us again at Wildwood, Florida. The new car conked out! It was night, we were out in the woods, it was dark and cold. We saw a light on the hill, and we went up to an old two-story wooden house and knocked on the door.

Some women were playing cards while their husbands had gone hunting. The lady who opened the door saw us, still dressed from the reception with rice on our clothes, and she guessed our situation. You never heard such a fuss. We couldn't get our car fixed because everything was closed for the holiday. They made us feel at home and offered us the master bedroom, where we spent the first night of our marriage. I'll never forget those kind women. Southern hospitality, they used to call it. When we finally saw a mechanic, he told us to drive slowly back to Tampa because they did not have the part that was needed to fix the car.

FERDIE: When they returned to Tampa the next night, it was New Year's Eve. The Columbia was jam-packed. They had not called ahead, so they came in and surprised their relatives.

Little Lawrence, an Annapolis graduate, son of Big Lawrence and a close cousin of Adela, was so happy to see her he went around hugging everyone. The problem was, he was a boxing champion at Annapolis and didn't know his strength; when he got to his Aunt Carmita, Adela's mother, he gave her the hardest hug of all and promptly broke her ribs.

It was, all things considered, a fitting end to the romance of Adela and Cesar.

CHICKEN
AND TURKEY

POLLO Y
PAVO

Baked Chicken à la Adela

Pollo al Horno à la Adela

1 4-lb. roasting chicken
Juice of 2 lemons
6 garlic cloves, mashed or pressed
Salt and pepper to taste

4 potatoes, boiled, peeled, and cut
    in ½-inch slices
Water or chicken broth

Wash chicken well, removing any pieces of kidney (sometimes left attached inside the body cavity). Bathe chicken with lemon juice, inside and outside. Rub chicken with garlic inside cavity, and outside and underneath the skin. Season with salt and pepper. If possible, marinate chicken overnight in the lemon and garlic. Tie legs together with string.

Place chicken, breast side down, in roasting pan in about ½ inch of water or chicken broth. Place roasting pan on lower rack of oven set on broil. Roast chicken uncovered at 400° about 50 minutes, always making sure that pan has ½ inch of water or broth. When chicken is brown, turn breast side up.

Remove chicken from pan and brown potatoes in pan juices under broiler. Cut chicken in quarters and serve with potatoes and pan juices. Serves 4.

Baked Chicken Garibaldi

Pollo Garibaldi

1 2½-lb. chicken
1 teaspoon minced garlic
20 sliced mushrooms
1 onion, cut in half-moon slices
1 green pepper, cut in half-moon
   slices
¼ cup grated Parmesan cheese

¼ cup red wine
2 cups chicken bouillon
½ cup grated toasted almonds
½ cup Spanish olive oil
1 tablespoon salt
Parsley leaves for garnish

Roast chicken at 400° for 30 minutes. Heat olive oil in skillet and sauté garlic, onion, and green pepper until onion is transparent. Add chicken bouillon and salt. When sauce begins to boil, add red wine and mushrooms. Cool and debone chicken; place in casserole. Spread sauce on top of chicken. Sprinkle Parmesan cheese over sauce. Bake at 350° for 30 minutes. Garnish with parsley leaves and almonds. Serves 2.

Chicken Alicante

Pollo Alicante

4 chicken breast halves
1 large onion, sliced
1 large green pepper, cut in rings
½ cup dry white wine
1 cup brown sauce (see p. 201)
¼ cup slivered almonds
4 slices eggplant

1 cup bread crumbs
1 egg, beaten
Flour
½ lb. cooked ham, cut in cubes
1 small can pineapple chunks
Salt and pepper to taste

Season chicken breasts with salt and pepper, place in 1 layer in baking dish, and cover with onion, green pepper, and brown sauce. Sprinkle slivered almonds on top and bake for 40 minutes at 450°, uncovered. While chicken is baking, fry sliced eggplant that has been floured, dipped in egg, and coated with bread crumbs. Skewer ham cubes and pineapple chunks alternately (about 3 of each); grill until light brown. Sprinkle wine over chicken when it comes out of the oven. Arrange chicken breasts on individual plates and garnish each serving with 1 slice of eggplant and 1 skewer of ham and pineapple. Serves 4.

Chicken in Black Sauce

Pollo en Salsa Negra

1 3½-lb. chicken (fryer), cut in
   8 pieces
1 teaspoon garlic powder
Juice of 1 lemon
¼ cup extra-virgin olive oil
1 large Spanish onion, chopped
1 teaspoon minced garlic
1 tablespoon flour

2 tablespoons red wine vinegar
1 cup chicken broth
2 bay leaves
2 teaspoons grated unsweetened
   chocolate
1 cup red wine
Salt and pepper to taste

Wash chicken, pat dry, and season with garlic powder, lemon juice, salt, and pepper. Heat oil in a deep casserole over medium heat. Brown chicken, remove from casserole, and set aside. In same oil, sauté onions until limp. Add garlic, being careful not to let it burn. Stir in flour. Add vinegar, wine, broth, and bay leaves; stir well. Return chicken to casserole, cover, and cook slowly for about 50 minutes. Remove chicken to a warm platter. Add chocolate to sauce and stir until chocolate is dissolved. Return chicken to casserole, baste with sauce, and simmer covered for 15 minutes. Serve with white rice or boiled new potatoes. Serves 4.

Chicken in a Blonde Sauce

Pollo en Salsa Rubia

1 3½-lb. chicken fryer, cut in
    8 pieces
¼ cup peanut oil
¼ cup olive oil
2 large Spanish onions, chopped
1 teaspoon chopped garlic
Salt and pepper to taste

1½ cups sliced mushrooms
2 bay leaves
3 medium potatoes, peeled and
    sliced in ½-inch-thick rounds
1 cup dry white wine
½ cup chicken broth
Dash sherry

Brown chicken in olive and peanut oil, in heavy-bottomed skillet with cover. Remove chicken and set aside. Sauté onions in same oil until golden. Add bay leaves, mushrooms, garlic, salt, and pepper. Return chicken to pan. Add wine and broth. Cover and cook over medium heat. When chicken is almost tender (about 25 minutes), add potato slices and cover. When potatoes are fork-tender (about 15 minutes), add sherry. Allow to stand about 15 minutes. Serve with fluffy white rice. Serves 4.

Chicken in a Casserole

Pollo Cacerola

1 2½-lb. whole chicken (fryer)
2 potatoes, peeled and sliced
½ medium onion, chopped
¼ cup sliced mushrooms
¼ cup sauterne
White pepper
2 tablespoons smoked ham, chopped

Pinch oregano
½ teaspoon garlic powder
3 chicken livers, chopped
¼ cup plus 2 tablespoons butter
½ teaspoon salt
Green peas (cooked) and parsley
    for garnish

Season chicken with oregano, garlic powder, and salt. Roast in 2 tablespoons butter for 30 minutes at 350° or until brown, basting several times. Remove chicken from oven. Strain gravy through colander. Heat ¼ cup butter in saucepan; sauté onion, ham, and livers, then add strained gravy from chicken. When onion is brown, remove from heat. Cut chicken into quarters, removing breastbone and thigh bones, and place in clay casserole. Add sauce, sliced potatoes, mushrooms, 2 tablespoons sauterne, and salt and pepper to taste. Bake 30 minutes at 350°. Sprinkle with remainder of sauterne. Garnish with peas and parsley. Serves 2.

Chicken Catalana

Pollo Catalana

1 2½-lb. chicken, cut in
   quarters
½ cup canned whole tomatoes,
   chopped
1 onion, chopped
½ cup Spanish olive oil
1 green pepper, chopped
20 mushrooms, sliced

3 cloves garlic, minced
1 teaspoon salt
¾ cup tomato sauce
Green peas (cooked), pimento or
   roasted red pepper strips, and
   chopped parsley for garnish
White wine

Heat oil in casserole or ovenproof skillet. Brown chicken. Add garlic, green pepper, and onion and sauté until green pepper is almost limp. Add tomato sauce and tomatoes. Bring to a boil; add salt and mushrooms. Cover and bake at 450° for 40–45 minutes. Garnish with pimentos, peas, and parsley. Sprinkle with white wine. Serves 2.

Chicken Diablo

Pollo al Diablo

6 chicken breast halves (skinless
   and boneless)
½ cup hot sauce
½ cup ketchup
1 cup sour cream

¼ teaspoon paprika
¼ cup honey
¼ teaspoon ground cumin
½ cup vegetable or peanut
   oil

In a bowl, mix hot sauce, honey, and sour cream until well blended. Add paprika, cumin, and ketchup and beat vigorously until sauce is well blended and smooth. Marinate chicken breast halves in half of sauce for at least 2 hours in refrigerator. Heat a heavy skillet or grill coated with vegetable oil. Brown breast halves on both sides in oil until cooked through (about 15 minutes) and serve with rest of sauce (heated). Serves 4.

Chicken Erasmo

Pollo Erasmo

½ chicken fryer or broiler, deboned
Juice of ½ lemon
4 round slices of potato, ½ inch
   thick
1 tablespoon olive oil
2 or 3 slices of onion
Pinch cumin seeds

2 slices fresh tomato
Pinch pepper
2 chicken livers
2 tablespoons white wine
1 tablespoon sliced mushrooms
Salt to taste

Broil chicken until light brown. On 12-inch square of aluminum foil, layer (in order) onion slices, potato slices, chicken, tomato slices, mushrooms. Place chicken livers on each side. Sprinkle with cumin seeds, pepper, salt, lemon juice, olive oil, and wine. Wrap snugly and bake in 450 to 500° oven for 25 minutes. Serves 1.

Chicken à la Father Hardy

Pollo à la Padre Hardy

1 2½-lb. whole chicken (fryer)
1 oz. cured ham, chopped
½ cup olive oil
½ tablespoon salt
½ Spanish onion, sliced in
　half-moons
24 toasted almonds

1 green pepper, sliced in half-rings
1½ cups chicken broth
4 chicken livers
½ cup champagne
8 rissolette potato balls (see
　below)
Chopped parsley

Roast chicken at 350° until brown (about 30 minutes). To make sauce, heat olive oil in saucepan and sauté onion, green pepper, ham, and chicken livers until peppers are limp. Season with salt. Add chicken broth. Place roasted chicken in casserole. Pour sauce over chicken, sprinkle almonds on top, and bake covered at 350° for 30 minutes. For approximately last 20 minutes of baking time, add rissolette potatoes to casserole, cover with sauce, and cook until fork-tender. (Make rissolette potatoes by scooping out balls from a raw Idaho potato with a melon ball cutter.) Sprinkle with champagne and garnish with chopped parsley. Serves 2.

Chicken Fricassee

Pollo Fricasé

1 3½-lb. chicken, cut in 8 pieces	2 bay leaves
Juice of 1 lemon	¼ cup olive oil
6 garlic cloves, minced	½ cup pitted green olives
2 potatoes, peeled and cut in chunks	½ cup raisins
2 onions, chopped	¼ cup capers
1 8-oz. can tomato sauce	½ cup sherry
¼ teaspoon ground cumin	Salt and pepper to taste

Marinate chicken in lemon juice, salt, and pepper for 2 hours. Heat olive oil in skillet or heavy-bottomed saucepan until a light haze forms over it. Brown chicken; add onions, garlic, bay leaves, cumin, and tomato sauce. When onions are almost tender, add potatoes, raisins, olives, and capers. Cook over low heat until chicken is tender. Stir in sherry. White rice is usually served as a side dish with fricassee. Serves 4–6.

Chicken in Garlic Sauce

Pollo al Ajillo

1 cup chicken tenders	6 2-inch red bell pepper strips
¼ cup crushed garlic	½ cup linguine, uncooked
¼ cup olive oil	2 tablespoons margarine
¼ cup sherry	Flour
⅓ cup brown sauce (see p. 201)	Romano cheese, grated
1 dried red chili pepper	(optional)
Juice of ½ lemon	Chopped parsley for garnish

Heat olive oil in skillet. Dust chicken tenders with flour. Sear chicken in olive oil to seal juices. Add garlic and continue to sauté. Add red bell peppers, chili pepper, and 2 tablespoons of margarine. Add sherry and lower heat. Add brown sauce and lemon juice and reduce sauce to desired thickness. Boil linguine al dente and place in 9-inch-wide rimmed soup bowl. Spoon chicken and sauce over top of pasta. Garnish with chopped parsley. A dash of Romano cheese may be added, if desired. Serves 1.

Chicken Livers Sauté

Hígados de Pollo Salteados

8 chicken livers	*Salt and pepper to taste*
3 tablespoons butter	*Flour*
½ small onion, chopped	*Parsley for garnish*
⅓ cup marsala or sherry	

In a skillet, sauté onion in butter until half-tender. Flour livers lightly and add to skillet. When livers are half done, add salt, pepper, and wine. Simmer for 15 minutes. Garnish with chopped parsley. Serves 1.

Chicken Liver Steak

Bistec de Hígados de Pollo

8 slices bacon
1 lb. chicken livers
¾ cup brown sauce (see p. 201)
¾ cup red wine

½ teaspoon garlic powder
Salt and pepper to taste
Tiny green peas (cooked) and
    chopped parsley for garnish

Season chicken livers with garlic powder, salt, and pepper. Divide into 2 portions and arrange each portion in the shape of a steak. Wrap bacon slices around livers, weaving and crisscrossing so livers will not separate. Pan-broil in heavy-bottomed skillet over medium heat for 15 minutes on each side. Combine brown sauce with red wine, heat, and add to chicken livers. Serve hot. Garnish with peas and parsley. Serves 2.

Chicken Marengo

Pollo al Marengo

1 2½-lb. chicken, cut in quarters
    and deboned
½ cup extra-virgin olive oil
1 cup flour
3 eggs, lightly beaten
1 Spanish onion, sliced

4 asparagus spears, preferably
    white
4 slices smoked ham
1 cup milk
½ cup white wine
Salt and pepper to taste
Chopped parsley for garnish

Salt and pepper chicken quarters, dip in beaten eggs, and coat with flour. Heat olive oil in skillet and brown chicken. Set aside.

Separate onion slices into rings. Dip onion rings, asparagus spears, and ham slices in milk and coat with flour. Fry all until golden. Serve hot chicken on platter decorated with onion rings, asparagus, and ham. Heat wine and pour over chicken; sprinkle with parsley. Serves 2.

Chicken Samuel

Pollo Samuel

4 chicken breast halves (skinless
   and boneless)
Juice of half a lemon
Garlic powder, salt, and pepper
   to taste
Flour
¼ cup extra-virgin olive oil

1 medium onion, chopped
2 shallots, chopped
2 garlic cloves, finely minced
½ cup sliced mushrooms
2 tablespoons flour
½ cup chicken broth
2 cups champagne or dry white
   wine

Pound chicken breast halves evenly to ½-inch thickness. Spread on platter. Season with lemon juice, garlic powder, salt, and pepper. Dust with flour and brown in oil in heavy skillet until cooked through. Remove from skillet and set aside. Sauté onion and shallots in same oil until wilted; add more oil if needed. Add garlic and mushrooms. Stir well and simmer for 2 minutes. Add 2 tablespoons flour and stir well. Add chicken broth and cook over medium heat until sauce thickens. Add wine and stir. Place chicken in ovenproof casserole, cover with sauce, and bake in a 400° oven for 5 minutes. Serves 2–4.

Chicken Sauté

Pollo Salteado

1½ lbs. boneless chicken breasts,
cut into bite-size pieces
1 green pepper, cut in strips
1 Spanish onion, cut in strips
1 cup potatoes, peeled and diced
2 ounces mushrooms, drained and
sliced
Salt and pepper to taste

½ cup brown sauce (see p. 201)
2 cloves fresh garlic, minced, or
1 teaspoon garlic powder
⅛ cup white wine
3 tablespoons Spanish olive oil
Vegetable or peanut oil for frying
potatoes

Fry diced potatoes in oil until done; set aside. Sauté onion and green pepper in olive oil till tender. Add chicken, salt, and pepper and sauté till done, over medium heat. Add mushrooms, brown sauce, garlic, and wine; simmer for 5 minutes. Serves 4.

Chicken and Yellow Rice

Arroz con Pollo

3-lb. chicken fryer, cut in quarters
2 onions, chopped
1 green pepper, chopped
2 medium tomatoes, peeled, seeded,
and chopped
2 cloves garlic, minced
½ cup olive oil
1 bay leaf
4 cups chicken broth

2 cups long-grain white rice,
uncooked
½ teaspoon saffron
½ tablespoon salt
½ cup small green peas (cooked)
4 asparagus tips
2 roasted red peppers, cut in strips
¼ cup white wine

In a skillet, sauté chicken in heated oil until skin is golden. Remove chicken and place in casserole. In same oil, sauté onion, green pepper, tomatoes, and garlic for 5 minutes. Pour over chicken. Add chicken broth, saffron, salt, bay leaf, and rice. When mixture begins to boil, cover casserole and bake in oven at 350° for 20 minutes or until chicken is done. Sprinkle with wine and garnish with peas, roasted red peppers, and asparagus tips. Serves 4.

Roast Turkey Cuban Style

Pavo Estilo Cubano

TURKEY

1 15-lb. young turkey	2 teaspoons pepper
1 cup sour orange juice (if not	12 garlic cloves, finely chopped
available, mix ½ cup lemon juice	Chicken broth or water for roasting
with ½ cup orange juice)	pan
2 teaspoons salt	

Pour juice over bird and inside cavity. Rub thoroughly with garlic, salt, and pepper inside and outside. This should be done 24 hours before roasting.

STUFFING

3 lbs. ground pork	2 cups dry sherry
3 lbs. ground beef	1 tablespoon salt
6 eggs, beaten lightly	1 tablespoon white pepper
½ cup pitted green olives	2 cups bread crumbs
½ cup raisins	1 cup toasted slivered almonds
½ cup capers	

Preheat oven to 325°. Combine all stuffing ingredients. Fill turkey cavity loosely with stuffing. Close cavity with trussing skewers or sew with trussing needle and thread. Place turkey, breast side up, in a roasting pan on a rack. Put ½ inch water or broth in pan; never let it dry up. Roast 3½ to 4 hours or until roasting thermometer inserted in thigh registers 175°; when turkey is golden, cover it loosely with aluminum foil. When done, transfer turkey to serving platter and allow it to stand 30 minutes. Remove trussing and serve. To make gravy, pour roasting pan juices into saucepan, boil, and correct for seasoning. Serves 8 to 10.

Chapter Eight

ADELA AND CESAR, NEWLYWEDS ON THE ROAD

FERDIE: The newlyweds settled in to enjoy life with a flourish. In 1948 Cesar was playing with his band at the Sapphire Room of Tampa's Floridian Hotel, and Adela was playing the piano in the Don Quixote. It was an idyllic time.

Cesar, now known professionally as Gonzmart, felt the need to assert himself, and he formed a society band to play in the best supper clubs in America. The band proved an immediate success, for the musicians were top-rate, the arrangements were well written, and the tall young Cesar was charismatic in his tie and tails, playing his violin and smiling seductively at the ladies.

Adela stayed in Tampa to deliver their first baby, a son named Cesar Casimiro Gonzmart. Four weeks later, mother and child joined the band business, and for the next four years their home was a hotel room or a cheap apartment. Adela, used to being spoiled at home, had not learned how to cook. Bright and adaptable, she learned fast.

ADELA: *I learned how to cook in a hurry. Luckily, Cesar was not finicky about food, and he was forgiving, for I learned to cook by the trial-and-error method. My mother gave me her recipes, and that's when I began collecting them. I still have that book full of handwritten notes on everything from soup to nuts.*

Most of the time we lived in hotels and small apartments where the kitchen was the size of a closet, and the pots and pans were inadequate.

In Virginia Beach we had a small apartment with a refrigerator that looked like it belonged in the Smithsonian Institution. It must have been the first model sold commercially. No washer or dryer either. I washed Casey's diapers in a four-legged tin tub and had a clothesline that unfortunately was strung under two trees. I say unfortunately because those two trees were home for hundreds of birds.

Glamour? I only went once to see Cesar and the band. The rest of the time I was learning how to cook, learning how to be a mother, and trying to learn how to be a wife.

We left Tampa and played in top-rated spots. We stayed three months at the Cavalier Hotel in Virginia Beach and then took a job in St. Louis at the Park Plaza.

By this time Casey was six months old, and we still called him "Baby." His first name was Cesar, but obviously it would be confusing to call him that. His second name was Casimiro, and a similar confusion existed. It took Liberace to break the logjam.

Liberace was the star of the show, with Cesar's band backing him up and playing for dancing. It was a very successful combination. Liberace's sister-in-law, wife of George, began calling the baby "Lover-baby," and soon everyone was calling him that. Well, I wasn't going to have this boy grow up with that handicap, so one day I decided that "Casey" would be his nickname. Cesar agreed, and to this day he is known as Casey, and definitely not "Lover-baby."

FERDIE: The show was a smash hit, and they stayed six months. By this time the gracious Liberace had been adopted by the young couple, and they decided to invite the young pianist to an elaborate Noche Buena party. It was to be a celebration of Christmas Eve like Cesar and Adela remembered from their days in Ybor City.

ADELA: *What a chore that was. First I had to ask the Columbia to send me black beans and plantains, which I could not find in St. Louis.*

We lived in a hotel-apartment that forbade cooking, so I had to bring in my groceries in a hatbox. What the doorman thought of me coming in and out repeatedly with a hatbox on one arm and six-month-old Casey on the other, I'll never know. I had to put damp towels around the doors so the smell of cooking onions and garlic wouldn't give us away. This came about because one morning I

Newlyweds at home, 1946. Their Lucy-Desi picture.

found a slip of paper under my door with a complaint from my next-door neighbor about the onion smell. It's a good thing they didn't have smoke alarms then. The towels did the job, and I continued my furious preparation to have a festive Noche Buena.

Since this apartment boasted no refrigeration, and since St. Louis winters were severe, I kept milk, butter, eggs, and other perishables on my windowsill.

Liberace and the guests had worked up a gigantic curiosity about spending a Cuban Noche Buena with us, and I was busy as a one-armed pianist, juggling my six-month-old baby, cooking, and finding the ingredients in local stores.

When the day arrived I realized that I was missing an essential item: Spanish cider. What is a Noche Buena feast without cider? I phoned every liquor store and supermarket to no avail. I was at wits' end when it occurred to me to call the Spanish consulate. Certainly they could help me.

A curt, serious voice answered the phone. It was the consul himself. Almost

Cesar Gonzmart and his Continental Society Orchestra in St. Louis, 1948.
He shared the stage with Liberace.

tearfully I blurted out my story, following Cesar's example and embellishing it as only he could. When I finished, there was a long pause, which I interpreted as a sigh.

"Lady, this is a consulate, a diplomatic service, not a grocery store."

The click on the other end indicated I had failed. Undaunted, Cesar went out and bought a case of Marqués de Riscal, wine from Spain. We nixed the cider. What Liberace didn't know wouldn't hurt him.

*The evening was splendid. By a stroke of luck, the **lechón,** beans, rice, and plantains were heavenly. Liberace could not conceal his joy as he came back for seconds, and Cesar was beaming with pride.*

To compliment me was not enough for the kind Liberace. Pulling me to his side, he sat at my small piano and, with the happy group of guests seated all around, played an emotional rendition of Brahms' "Lullaby" in honor of our child, Casey, who was snoozing contentedly in his crib, oblivious to the musical honor being played to him by one of America's top entertainers.

When he was finished, he pulled me down on the piano bench, and I felt that I had to return his beautiful gift of music. I played Lecuona's "Malagueña" and the lilting "La Comparsa," which I felt this Cuban evening deserved. Liberace led the applause. I was in heaven.

It was on this emotional high that Cesar went to work the next night. Unfortunately, Scrooge was alive and well in St. Louis. That night the owner gave Cesar two weeks' notice. We got canned on Christmas night.

Still, as Bogey says, "We'll always have St. Louis," for no one can take away the fun and emotion of that Noche Buena. The best of my entire life.

Ferdie: Christmas Eve—Noche Buena in Ybor City—was the most important family night of the year. Latins celebrate this event as the high point of the Christmas holidays; so, growing up in a multicultural society, we children got a double bonus. On Christmas Eve we celebrated with our Latin families, and on Christmas Day we could celebrate with our Anglo friends.

In medieval times, holidays were the only days that the peasants got to eat the food they raised solely for sale. Their daily meals were skimpy, mainly porridge and gruel. But on high holidays, of which Christmas Eve was first and foremost, they were entitled to eat the "luxury" foods; therefore, the holiday recipes date back to the time when peasants waited the entire year to eat in splendor.

Any immigrant society tends to bond together in the new land, and the citizens of Ybor City were no exception. In addition to division by nationality, groups of families tended to live side by side or within the same block.

Adela: *My father lived in Ybor City, a few blocks from the Columbia. He felt it was a practical consideration, for he could walk to work and therefore did not need to buy a car. We usually had members of my mother's family living near us. Across the street from us lived my father's brother and his wife, Lawrence and Gloria, who had two children, my cousins Lorencito and Casey. We were in each other's homes constantly. On Christmas Eve it was one happy merry-go-round as we not only visited Lawrence and Gloria but had an open house for the neighbors, who also had their own open houses.*

Ferdie: One of the best memories I have of that night, besides the heavenly aroma of the food, the coffee, and the *puros* (cigars), was the magical camaraderie it generated. Feuds, grudges, and arguments were forgotten. A blanket of good feeling covered the evening. If a family boasted good storytellers—and every Ybor City family seemed to have at least one—laughter

Liberace and Cesar, 1948. A great Spanish Christmas Eve was
in store for Liberace.

filled the house, and one story brought on another. As a child I was fascinated
to hear the stories of the past and to see serious men convulsed in laughter.

My Uncle Paulino was a great storyteller and seemed to have a story for
each event. He also had a fanciful answer for every question he was asked, an
answer that everyone knew he was making up on the spur of the moment. For
example, on being asked about *plátanos,* Paulino told this story about how
the banana-like vegetable got its name:

"In the days of the conquest of the New World we used to send the gold
and silver back to Spain in galleons. Some also contained the fruits, vegetables, and foodstuffs of the countries they were occupying.

"The French and English pirates raided the sea lanes, looking for ships carrying gold and silver. They did not need the food ships except to reprovision themselves.

"When the galleons made port in Cádiz, the poor would line the wharves, arms outstretched, begging for a coin of gold, *oro,* or silver, *plata.*

"People on ships carrying plátanos would throw them to the people, yelling as they passed by: 'Plata-no, plata-no,' meaning no silver. Just bananas.

"And from that time on, bananas became known in Spain as *plátanos.*"

Laughter was accompanied by raised eyebrows. I have sold that story to several historical journals as historic fact. This was in the days when I was paying my way through college.

A D E L A : *In our neighborhood Noche Buena wasn't complete until El Gaitero, the bagpiper man, came by and played a tune and had his drink. Bagpipes are common in the north of Spain where seafaring Scotsmen raided the northern coast. Where this man came from I never found out.*

He would go from house to house, boisterously welcomed, playing enthusiastically, drinking heartily until he could go no farther because of the drink—giving rise to the now popular motto "Don't drink while playing bagpipes."

F E R D I E : The adopted style for Noche Buena was a sit-down dinner for one's family, then a buffet of fruits, cheeses, desserts, wines, aperitifs, brandies, liqueurs, *turrones,* and expresso for visitors.

Later, when prosperity brought us wheels, we would travel all over Ybor City to visit friends as well as relatives. It went on into the morning and was truly a joyous punctuation for the year.

The three principal immigrant groups each had their own distinctive and well-defined menu. As the years passed, and intermarriage and Americanization blurred these dietary distinctions, the Noche Buena feast became more eclectic, so that now a Spaniard roasts a pig, an Italian eats *bollinas,* and a Cuban can serve spaghetti with his main course.

A D E L A : *I have compiled three basic Noche Buena menus. These are popular menus of the early days of Ybor City, representing the three major nationalities in Ybor City and showing how their cuisines differed.*

An interesting problem arose while I was writing these menus. I was always told that the Catholic Church had issued a special dispensation for the Spanish people because of their expulsion of the Moors. They could eat meat on any day they wished. The rest of the Catholic world could not eat meat on Fridays and certain holidays. Therefore, most of my Italian friends featured fish on Christmas Eve.

In doing deeper research I found that the Italians of Ybor City divided themselves into Sicilians and mainland Italians. The Sicilians ate fish, the mainland Italians meat, fowl, or fish. So, in the interest of completeness and accuracy, I am listing both versions.

A SPANISH CHRISTMAS EVE

The meal started officially with the serving of chicken soup, which could be a clear soup or a soup with vermicelli, potatoes, and pieces of chicken. Spaniards did not serve salads as such, although sliced tomatoes were to be had if desired.

The main meal was a roast chicken with small, round roasted potatoes surrounding the golden bird. Some families favored a stuffing, but the majority just roasted chickens. In some houses they also served a red snapper, but that was not a required course.

Some houses bought a serrano ham, which is a cured ham, similar to Italian prosciutto. This is served in thin slices with white or yellow cheese.

*Many families, particularly those from Asturias, liked to end the meal with roasted chestnuts, marzipan, **bollinas,** and **sidra,** a fermented apple cider that resembles champagne. **Bollinas** were small turnovers of dough filled with chopped walnuts, sugar, honey, and cinnamon, and fried.*

*Every house boasted a delicious assortment of **turrones,** hard or soft bars of almond and nougat mixtures. The hard candy **alicante** had a thin rice-paper covering that resembled a communion host wafer. It was edible, but this was a matter of taste. The soft bars were made of ground almonds and honey and had the same consistency as guava paste. The best of these had egg yolks added and was called **turron de yema.** They are still available and widely enjoyed today in Ybor City and Hispanic communities throughout the United States.*

***Membrillo** was a paste made from quince and sugar, which was eaten with white cheese to cut the heavy sweetness.*

*Dessert also featured a spectacular **brazo gitano,** basically a sponge cake roll* with a cream filling. It was covered with a clear, simple syrup made with sherry, sugar, and lemon peel and topped with meringue.

Expresso coffee topped the meal, with sides of Spanish brandies as desired.

All Spanish Noche Buenas had two ingredients in common: Cuban bread, freshly baked, and **puros** for after-dinner smokes.

After dinner the men told stories or played dominoes or cards until it was time to retire.

A Cuban Christmas Eve

The Cuban Christmas Eve was more festive and relaxed, perhaps because of the weather. Christmas in Cuba is still balmy enough to be celebrated out of doors.

*The main dish was a whole **lechón** (pig) roasted on an open fire. This was constantly turning. The pig was basted with **mojo**, a mixture of sour orange juice, garlic, oregano, and bay leaves. As the **lechón** rotated on its spit, guava leaves were placed on the fire, imparting a delicious aroma to the fire and obviously to the **lechón**.*

The Cuban Noche Buena differed from the European in that it did not come one course at a time but, like a tropical storm, hit with full force all at once.

The Cubans wasted very little time with appetizers or soup. If they wished, black beans could be served as soup, but most preferred it as part of the main meal.

The Cubans love their rum and good music, and they are always fashionably late to serve the main course, which leaves ample time to drink, dance, and socialize. Noche Buena was a time of relaxation, a celebration of joy, and no one was in a hurry to eat on schedule.

*The main course, and the only course in most houses, came served on a large plate. The guests chose the pieces of meat they desired from the **lechón**, and it was carved in front of them. Then a bewildering variety of tasty foods were placed on the plate beside the **lechón**, which had been doused in **mojo**.*

*On the other side of the plate was a white, pulpy, delicious vegetable called **yuca**, spelled **yucca** in English, which grows all over Cuba and now in Florida. It is a root, like a potato but quite stringy. It is almost the equivalent of mashed potatoes when cooked, but it has a different consistency and taste. Some love to put lemon on it. It was also served with **mojo**.*

Around the borders of the plate were long slices of succulent, sweet, fried **plátanos maduros** (ripe plantains).

An advantage to backyard cooking was the by-product, the crisp, roasted fragments of pork skin. It is called crackling in English, **crispito** or **chicharrones** in Spanish, and the chosen few got this treasure.

There was usually tomato and watercress salad and, if in season, avocados. The dressing was invariably olive oil and vinegar.

Cubans enjoyed Spanish cider, as well as white or red wine from Europe. Beer was also very popular.

The Cubans were great bread eaters, and in Ybor City they found the most savory bread in the world. Some liked to eat Cuban lard crackers.

For dessert, guava was presented either as a paste, served with white or yellow cheese, or as a sweet preserve of the rind in thick sugary syrup, served with cream cheese and Cuban lard crackers to cut the sweetness. Roasted chestnuts and a variety of nuts, almonds, and fresh fruit were available. So were **turrones** from Spain; the favorite was **turron de yema.**

Membrillo was as popular in Cuba as it was in Spain. Probably the Cubans got the idea of making guava paste from **membrillo,** which resembles guava paste except that it is made from quince.

Liqueurs came with the **café solo,** or expresso. The favorite was Anis del Mono, a Spanish anisette, but there were those who preferred Spanish brandy. **Sidra asturiana** (Spanish cider) was also enjoyed.

Of course, the final touch was a giant **puro,** made by hand in the factories of Ybor City.

An Italian Christmas Eve

In Ybor City it was difficult to say what was a typical Italian Christmas Eve, for this group was divided into Sicilians and mainland Italians. Herein I attempt to present a typical Italian Christmas Eve, combining the two, using the dishes that both had in common.

The night started with appetizers: **caponata,** a pickled eggplant (easy to make and very tasty), and plates of sliced sausage, cheeses, and anchovies. They usually ate lightly here, so they would come to the dinner table ready to eat.

A favorite olive dish was called **olivi scacciate,** or cracked olive salad, featuring celery, garlic, olive oil, and vinegar over a variety of cut olives, black and green, from Italy and Greece.

Italians served a red wine which they had made in October. The cask was opened in December for Christmas Eve. In this they differed from the rest of Ybor City: Spaniards and Cubans favored bottled red and white wines from Europe.

The meal started with a small plate of soup, sometimes minestrone, made from fresh vegetables, although many liked chicken broth with vermicelli noodles better.

The pasta dish followed, with different kinds of pasta favored by different houses: bucatini, linguine, spaghetti, macaroni, coditos, mezzani, dilatini, and shells.

The pasta varied but the sauce generally did not. It was a tomato-based sauce made from canned Italian tomatoes, slowly cooked for three hours. Then a meat, which had been fast-fried, locking in the blood, was added along with garlic, onion, and basil, and the sauce simmered for an hour more.

Some Sicilians maintain they only ate fish, and some Italians maintain they had either turkey, chicken, or meat. Most in Ybor City agree that they never saw a turkey served, but would broil chickens and potatoes as the main course. Leg of veal was also a favorite. Diagonal holes were drilled into the leg of veal, then filled with onion, garlic, and oregano. The veal was roasted slowly in the oven and served sliced, with small onions and potatoes.

Some, remembering the ways of the old country, bought a young goat, called a **crasto,** and cooked it over an open fire, like the Cubans cook their **lechón.** While it rotated on its spit it was basted with **mojo** sauce, which was identical to the Cuban variety except that Italians added mint.

For some, the main dish was a freshly caught red snapper, called **pargo.** The fish was gutted, and the empty cavity was filled with a stuffing made of lobster, shrimp, crab, celery, and condiments such as finely chopped fresh parsley, onion, garlic, tomato, and basil. The fish was then closed with toothpicks or sewn together and baked, basted in a preheated mixture of olive oil and butter, with a pinch of garlic added. It was served whole, with the head and tail in place, and cut in cross-sections. It was garnished with parsley and served with its stuffing and halves of lemon. Some liked to serve an artichoke stuffed with cheese as a side dish.

After the meal, while the women cleared the table, pieces of Italian sausage and a special stuffed sausage from Sicily were served along with a dish of varied nuts.

Struffoli was a favorite dessert. It was made by rolling masses of dough in the palm of one hand, which was coated with honey. These were then rolled into pine-cone-like configurations, the honey serving to hold them together, and covered with colored sprinkles. The honey-covered balls were carefully stuck one on top of the other to form a Christmas tree that was a delectable delight.

Cassata were Sicilian cakes with a creamy middle, covered with real whipped cream. **Cannolis** (cream rolls) were available, along with **turrones** from Italy, which are very similar to Spanish **turrones**. There was also fresh fruit accompanied by a variety of cheeses.

Expresso coffee was served with a side tumbler of anisette, with a coffee bean floating inside. Those who did not prefer to drink the liqueur could use an anisette stick to stir their coffee.

The men usually played cards after dinner, either **chicknetta** (a form of poker), hearts, or straight poker. Those with big enough yards played **bocce**, a ball game, but few had such accommodations because their homes were small.

The Italian colony was well served by several excellent grocery stores which carried Italian and Sicilian products. All nationalities preferred Italian olive oil, cheeses, and olives, green and black. The most popular stores for Italian foodstuffs were the Cacciatore Family Grocery on Seventh Avenue, Demmi's Import on Seventh Avenue between Eighteenth and Nineteenth Streets, Agliano Fish Market on Seventh Avenue, Castellano and Pizzo on Eighth Avenue and Nineteenth Street, and Alessi Bakeries in West Tampa.

Cuban Bread, Spanish Custard (Flan), Sangria, Grouper à la Rusa, Cuban Sandwich.
Photo by Sam Cranston, courtesy of *The News-Journal*, Daytona Beach, Fla.

Red Snapper Amandine.

Cream-Filled Roll (Brazo Gitano).

Chicken and Yellow Rice. Photo by Sam Cranston, courtesy of *The News-Journal*, Daytona Beach, Fla.

1905 Salad.

Paella
Valenciana.

Snapper Alicante. Photo by Sam Cranston, courtesy of *The News-Journal*, Daytona Beach, Fla.

Spanish Bean Soup.

SAUCES

❀

SALSAS

Brown Sauce (Spanish Sauce)

Salsa Española

¼ cup beef drippings
1 tablespoon butter
1 onion, chopped
1 carrot, chopped
1 stalk celery, chopped
½ teaspoon thyme
1 tablespoon minced smoked ham
¼ cup flour

1 cup tomato puree
5 peppercorns
4 cups beef stock
¼ cup parsley, coarsely chopped
¼ cup Madeira wine
1 bay leaf
Salt to taste

Melt beef drippings and butter in saucepan. Sauté vegetables, bay leaf, thyme, and ham. Add flour and cook mixture until over medium heat until flour is light brown. Add tomato puree, peppercorns, beef stock, and parsley. Cook over low heat, covered, for 2 hours. Add wine. Season with salt to taste. This sauce is used as a base for many dishes. Makes about 3 cups.

Catalana Sauce

Salsa Catalana

1 28-oz. can tomato sauce
1 28-oz. can crushed tomatoes
4 onions, chopped
4 green peppers, cut in strips
2 bay leaves
4 garlic cloves, finely minced

½ cup extra-virgin olive oil
1 teaspoon sugar
1 teaspoon paprika
Salt and pepper to taste
1 quart water

Sauté onions and green peppers in olive oil. Add garlic, tomatoes, and tomato sauce. Add bay leaves, paprika, sugar, and water. Cook over medium heat for 1 hour. Add salt and pepper. Makes about 2 quarts.

Coruñesa Sauce

Salsa Coruñesa

2 onions, chopped

3 carrots, scraped and chopped

1 stalk celery, chopped

6 garlic cloves, finely minced

2 blue crabs, shelled and cut up
   in small pieces

1 teaspoon paprika

⅛ teaspoon yellow food coloring

2 teaspoons salt

2 quarts water

2 tablespoons flour

1 stick butter

¼ cup olive oil

½ cup white wine

¼ cup brandy

1 16-oz. can tomato sauce

1 teaspoon Pernod

1 teaspoon white pepper

Melt butter and olive oil in large saucepan. Sauté onions, celery, carrots, and garlic. Add tomato sauce, crab, paprika, and flour. Stir well and add water. Boil gently for 30 minutes. Strain through a fine sieve and add food coloring. Return to pot and add wine, brandy, Pernod, salt, and pepper. Makes about 2 quarts.

Cuban Garlic Sauce

Mojito Salsa

8 garlic cloves
1 teaspoon salt
1 medium onion, thinly sliced
½ cup extra-virgin olive oil

½ cup sour orange juice (or ½ cup
    orange juice combined with
    ½ cup lemon juice)

Crush garlic with salt in a mortar and pestle or in a food processor until it forms a smooth paste. Combine garlic, onion, and orange juice in a bowl. Heat oil in skillet, add mixture, and stir for 3 minutes. This sauce can be used immediately or stored in refrigerator and reheated. Makes 1 cup.

Garlic Salad Dressing

Salsa de Ajo

½ cup white vinegar
1½ cups extra-virgin olive oil
2 teaspoons salt
¼ teaspoon pepper

1 teaspoon dry mustard
4 garlic cloves, finely minced
1 teaspoon oregano

Mix all ingredients thoroughly with wire whisk. Serve at room temperature. Makes 2 cups.

Spaghetti Sauce # 1

Salsa de Tomate # 1

6 scallions without tops, chopped
6 garlic cloves, chopped
¼ cup extra-virgin olive oil
1 32-oz. can crushed tomatoes
1 32-oz. can tomato sauce

1 carrot, scraped and sliced
8 fresh sweet basil leaves,
   or ½ teaspoon dried basil
Salt and pepper to taste

Sauté scallions and garlic in olive oil until limp. Add crushed tomatoes, tomato sauce, carrot, basil, salt, and pepper. Cook, partially covered, for approximately 1 hour. Makes about 2 quarts.

Spaghetti Sauce # 2

Salsa de Tomate # 2

6 scallions without tops, chopped
1 teaspoon minced garlic
¼ cup extra-virgin olive oil

3 pounds plum tomatoes, peeled
   and seeded
8 sweet basil leaves

Sauté scallions and garlic in olive oil until limp. Process tomatoes in food processor until coarsely chopped. Add to scallions and garlic. Add sweet basil and boil gently, partially covered, for 30 minutes. Makes about 4 cups.

PASTA

Pasta Coruñesa

10 large shrimps, peeled and
    deveined (tails off)
1 onion, chopped
1 green pepper, chopped
¼ cup crabmeat, cooked
½ garlic clove, minced
2 tablespoons brandy

2 tablespoons white wine
⅓ cup Coruñesa sauce (see p. 202)
2 tablespoons olive oil
Salt and pepper to taste
½ cup linguine, uncooked
Chopped parsley
Romano cheese (optional)

Heat olive oil in skillet. Add onion, green pepper, garlic, and shrimp. Sauté for 2 minutes. Add brandy and flambé. Add white wine and Coruñesa sauce. Simmer to reduce by half. Add crabmeat, salt, and pepper last. Boil linguine al dente. Heat sauce through, pour over pasta, and garnish with parsley. If desired, sprinkle with Romano cheese. Serves 1.

Pasta with Crab in White Sauce

Pasta con Jaiba en Salsa Blanca

2 lbs. lump crabmeat, picked over
    to remove foreign particles
1 onion, finely chopped
2 shallots, finely chopped
1 teaspoon chopped garlic
1 stick butter
Grated Parmesan cheese to taste

½ cup extra-virgin olive oil
½ cup clam broth
½ cup white wine
½ teaspoon white pepper
Salt to taste
¼ cup chopped parsley
1 lb. linguine, uncooked

Sauté onion, shallots, and garlic in butter and olive oil until limp. Add crabmeat; toss lightly. Add, in order, clam broth, wine, salt, pepper, and parsley. Boil linguine al dente and drain. Ladle sauce over linguine. Sprinkle with Parmesan cheese. Serves 4.

Pasta, Meatball, and Broccoli Casserole

Pasta con Albóndigas y Broccoli en Cacerola

MEATBALLS

1 lb. ground beef

2 eggs

¾ cup bread crumbs

½ cup grated Romano cheese

½ cup water

1 teaspoon finely minced garlic

½ cup peanut oil

Salt and pepper to taste

1 qt. Spaghetti Sauce # 1
  (see p. 204)

Beat eggs with cheese, garlic, bread crumbs, and water. Add meat, salt, and pepper and mix well. Form into balls (about the size of a golf ball). Brown lightly in oil and drain. Cook for 20 minutes in spaghetti sauce.

BROCCOLI

1 16-oz. bag frozen broccoli cuts

2 teaspoons finely minced garlic

½ cup extra-virgin olive oil

Salt and pepper to taste

Cook broccoli according to package directions. Drain. In a large frying pan, sauté garlic in olive oil. Add broccoli, salt, and pepper and cook over medium heat for 2 to 3 minutes. Set aside.

ASSEMBLING CASSEROLE

½ lb. ziti or rotelli pasta, uncooked

Meatballs in sauce

Broccoli mixture

⅔ cup grated Romano cheese

Boil pasta al dente and drain. Remove meatballs from sauce. Spread a third of the sauce in bottom of large rectangular casserole dish. Follow with a layer of pasta, a third of the sauce, then all the broccoli. Sprinkle half of cheese over broccoli. Add another layer of pasta. Break up meatballs slightly with a fork and spread over pasta. Add last third of sauce, then rest of cheese. Cover with aluminum foil and bake at 400° for 10 minutes. Serves 8.

Vegetables

�֍

Verduras

Plantains Temptation

Plátanos Tentación

4 ripe plantains
½ stick butter
½ cup light brown sugar

1 cinnamon stick, or ½ teaspoon
   ground cinnamon
½ cup cream sherry

Peel plantains and slice in half lengthwise. Melt butter in skillet over low heat. Add sugar, cinnamon stick, and sherry; stir. Add plantains, coat with mixture, and cover skillet. Cook over low heat, turning plantains occasionally until they are caramel-colored. Serve warm or at room temperature; do not refrigerate, as plantains will harden. Serves 4.

Stuffed Artichokes

Alcachofa Rellena

4 artichokes
2 cups ground smoked ham or
   chopped cooked shrimp
2 cups bread crumbs
1 cup chopped parsley
16 garlic cloves, minced
2 shallots, finely chopped

½ cup grated Romano cheese
1 cup extra-virgin olive oil
½ teaspoon black pepper
2 tablespoons vinegar or lemon juice
2 medium potatoes, cubed
1 carrot, sliced
6 parsley sprigs

Trim tops of artichoke leaves with scissors. Slice stem evenly, making sure that artichoke will stand erect. Trim stems with vegetable parer. In a big pot, boil 3 to 4 quarts of salted water with 2 tablespoons of vinegar or lemon juice. Boil artichokes and stems for ten minutes. Remove from water and drain. When cool enough to handle, spread leaves and remove as much as possible of fuzz at bottom of artichoke.

To make filling, combine thoroughly ham or shrimp, bread crumbs, parsley, 10 minced garlic cloves, shallots, cheese, pepper, and ½ cup oil. Stuff center and leaves with filling. Place artichokes in Dutch oven in an inch of water, ½ cup oil, 6 crushed garlic cloves, and 6 sprigs of parsley. Cover with tight-fitting lid and simmer over low heat. Braise cubed potatoes and carrot slices in water until tender. When artichokes are tender (after approximately 1½ hours or when leaves can be pulled out easily), remove from stove. Transfer artichokes to serving platter and serve nestled in potatoes and carrots. Serves 4.

Stuffed Green Peppers

Ajíes Rellenos

4 large green peppers	*1 lb. ground chuck*
2 slices bread, cubed	*1 16-oz. can tomatoes, drained*
1 large onion, chopped	*and chopped (reserve juice)*
1 teaspoon salt	*¼ teaspoon pepper*
2 tablespoons Worcestershire sauce	*¾ cup ketchup*

Wash green peppers, cut off stem end, and remove seeds and membrane. Parboil peppers 5 minutes in enough boiling salted water to cover peppers. Drain and set aside. Sauté onion and beef. Add drained tomatoes. Mix bread cubes, Worcestershire sauce, salt, pepper, and ½ cup ketchup; combine with beef mixture. Stuff peppers and place in baking pan. Combine reserved tomato juice and ¼ cup ketchup. Pour over peppers, cover, and bake at 300° for 1 hour. Serves 4.

Stuffed Eggplant

Berenjena Rellena

1 large eggplant	½ cup bread crumbs
1 egg, lightly beaten	4 tablespoons butter
2 tablespoons chopped shallots	Grated Romano or Parmesan cheese
½ cup cooked crabmeat	1 tablespoon capers
1 teaspoon chopped parsley	½ cup cooked, chopped shrimp

Cut eggplant in half lengthwise and bake at 400° until fork-tender. Scoop out pulp. In skillet, brown shallots in butter. Season and add pulp of eggplant, shrimp, egg, parsley, capers, and crabmeat. Mix well; stuff eggplant halves. Sprinkle with bread crumbs and cheese. Bake at 350° until brown (15–20 minutes). Serves 2.

White Bean Torte

Munyeta

1½ lbs. great northern beans, dried	4 garlic cloves, minced
2 **chorizos** (Spanish sausages), sliced	¼ lb. smoked ham, finely diced
2 medium onions, finely chopped	½ cup extra-virgin olive oil
⅛ lb. salt pork, finely diced	Salt and pepper to taste

Soak beans overnight. Drain, cover with more water, add a little salt, and boil until beans are tender. Drain, reserving liquid. In large skillet, sauté salt pork, ham, *chorizos*, onions, and garlic until onions are transparent. Add beans, pepper, and salt, if needed. Sprinkle with small amount of cooking liquid from beans. Cook slowly until brown on bottom. Remove by using a large inverted plate. Add a little oil to pan and brown torte on other side. Invert onto a plate, let stand for 5 minutes, and cut into wedges. Serves 6.

Chapter Nine

ℛETURN TO THE
Columbia

ADELA: *We had been touring for years, and I was getting weary of life on the road. Frankly, the time had passed so fast that I couldn't find a point at which I could say "No más" to Cesar.*

Leave it to a child to bring you to your senses. One day, when we had been closed up in our hotel room in Chicago during one of their arctic winters, little Casey came to me with tears in his huge, beautiful black eyes.

"Mama, don't they have grass in this city?"

Poor Casey was four years old. He'd had no playmate but me, had spent his winters in hotel rooms, and was growing up like a gypsy with no sense of home and family. No roots.

Well, that was it! That brought everything into focus. When Cesar came home I told him how I felt. I had to go home. I wanted to live in Tampa, surrounded by family and friends. I wanted Casey to know his grandfather and to grow up near the Columbia, as I had.

Cesar and his band were riding high and were booked for the opening of the Caribe Hilton in Puerto Rico. It was a choice engagement, and the contract was for a lot of money for a long stay.

I did not suggest that he give it up. I told him to go do the engagement and come to Tampa and visit us when he could. By himself, on his own, Cesar arrived at the conclusion that it was time to return to Ybor City and provide Casey with a proper home. He turned down the contract. We were going home.

FERDIE: By this time some dramatic and tragic changes had occurred at the Columbia Restaurant.

With the death of Lawrence Hernandez the partnership landed in the hands of his heir, Little Lawrence, at that time a naval officer. Getting out of the navy was easy, since the navy was top-heavy with officers in the years following World War II. Lawrence returned, determined to take over as a full partner. He brought with him a wife who was far from an ordinary bride.

Libby was a southern belle of the Scarlett O'Hara variety. Beautiful outside and flinty tough inside. Her relationship with Lawrence was explosive, and it didn't take a degree in psychiatry to know this would end badly.

At that time Casimiro decided to expand. He opened a second Columbia in the airport at Orlando, and he sent Cesar to learn the business of restaurant management. It was good basic training, for the restaurant was small and Orlando was a small village, in the days before the Mouse changed the economy of Florida. Disneyland was in the future. While in Orlando, Adela became pregnant again and delivered another strong boy. This one got a name right away: Ricardo Orlando Gonzmart. It's a good thing the restaurant wasn't in Wymauma.

The expansion of the Orlando restaurant was blocked by political factors, and there was no alternative but to close. It had served its purpose: it gave Cesar time to make the transition from the glamour of show business to the tough life of running a restaurant.

By the time Cesar returned to the Columbia in Ybor City, a tragic event had occurred that changed all their lives. The combative couple, Lawrence and Libby, had brought their disaster of a marriage to a head on a hot summer night in the early 1950s. Libby, tired of being physically abused, shot Lawrence. The shooting did not take his life, but it paralyzed him from the waist down. He survived for two more years before he died on a visit to Havana. Shortly thereafter his mother, the widow Gloria, expired of a heart attack. This left the kindly Casey as a survivor.

The Columbia Restaurant was in the sole hands of Casimiro, the man who had created the highly successful business. Lawrence, Jr., Gloria, and Casey had sold their share of the restaurant to him some years before. He was now grooming his successor, Cesar.

Adela, Cesar, Casey, and Richard, 1955. The young family
is complete.

It was an odd coupling: Casimiro, the taciturn, tough taskmaster, conservative in money matters, struggling to keep his restaurant at its high level of quality, trying to teach Cesar, who was mercurial, a dreamer, a visionary, an artist, a man for whom money was merely a ticket to his next dream. To say poor Cesar was frustrated during this hard apprenticeship is an understatement.

Casimiro never tired of saying, "Cesar is a great racehorse, but he needs a jockey to hold him back." It was as succinct and accurate a description of the young, ambitious Cesar Gonzmart as I ever heard.

ADELA: *It was so tough on Cesar, being the boss's son-in-law. He was determined to learn, to show the naysayers that he could win over the Columbia employees. It took years. He turned a deaf ear; he turned insults into jokes. When a waiter ridiculed his unfashionably long hair, Cesar said, "I'm a violinist. What's your excuse?"*

By the time my father died, Cesar was well liked and accepted. He had paid dearly, but he had persevered. He knew the restaurant business, and now he had the opportunity to save the Columbia from the decline and dry rot that was turning Ybor City into a ghost town. The Columbia, at the end of the streetcar line, was about to wither and die. Good food in glamorous surroundings wasn't enough. Something more was needed. Cesar knew exactly what it was.

On trips to Miami, we visited old friends we had known in Cuba. The refugees from Castro's takeover were pouring into Miami. They were the top class of political exiles. Some brought their money and jewels with them. Pepe and Albino Currais, whose family had owned La Zaragozana and The 1830 in Havana, were among them. The brothers decided to open a supper club on Biscayne Boulevard, halfway between Little Havana and Miami Beach. They called it Les Violins, and it immediately became a phenomenal success. When Cesar saw their achievement, he decided that since there was nothing like that in Tampa he would put this same type of entertainment in the Columbia.

What Cesar set about to do was to save both the restaurant and his professional pride. Also, he missed performing. Cesar was a performer, first, last, and to the end of his days.

He started modestly enough, with an accordionist named Pego and three Cuban violinists. They strolled among the diners in the Quixote and the Patio. They went over big.

Then one night while I sat watching these musicians, I got a flash in my mind. What was lacking? Charisma. A leader with a continental charm. A musician who was superior to these four. I found I was describing Cesar.

That night I told Cesar he had to go back to the violin. He initially begged off, but I could see he had the same idea. He set off to practice as if he had a concert to perform at Carnegie Hall.

Cesar's strolling violins were exactly what we needed to set us off from other places. We offered fine food in glamorous settings with a continental flavor. It was different. It was right. It was good.

Cesar had worked hard and had now found his niche. A tough businessman by day, he was a star at night. The Columbia was saved and continued to do well while all of Ybor City was disintegrating.

I continued to do occasional concert dates, but eventually I retired to be a wife and mother following a stint on the new media gadget, television. Cesar fashioned a half-hour program, calling it **Latin Quarter Review.** *It was a solid half-hour at six o'clock on Tampa's WFLA Channel 8. It featured Cesar and his violin, his society orchestra, me at the piano as a soloist, and entertainers who were appearing at the Columbia. The addition of guest shots by popular young Latin entertainers from Tampa, such as the comic Jack Espinosa and a beautiful young singer, Dalia Fernandez, brought more viewers to the show. It was very popular, and we were fully sponsored. One sponsor sold chinchillas. My, what sponsors Cesar would find! We had a lot of fun, but at the end I came to an unexpected conclusion.*

My performing days were over. I didn't need a Steinway to hit me on the head. There is only room for one star in a family, and in my family Cesar Gonzmart was the star. He had earned it. He deserved it. We had bought a beautiful home on prestigious Davis Island and paid $23,000 for it. It was time to dedicate myself to making an attractive home for Cesar and our two growing boys.

Now, as I write this, I'm more certain than ever that I was right.

FERDIE: After the war Tampa began to explode with growth. In the shabby area of the downtown business district, the politicians built a large convention center, and it began to attract large groups to Tampa. Cesar saw the need to expand the Columbia by building a showroom that would seat three hundred. Casimiro, ever the cautious businessman, was not enthusiastic. Where Cesar saw the increase of population and conventioneers, Casimiro saw the loss of regular customers through aging and death and the disappearance of Ybor City as an immigrant society.

A large rectangular room was built, adjacent to the Patio. It had none of the Columbia's trademark elegance and architectural uniqueness. It was a simple, modern room, built specifically to showcase entertainers.

The Siboney Room, the new room built to feature entertainment, 1955.

In an effort to make the room unique, Cesar brought in a famous Spanish muralist, Teok Carrasco, to do a series of panels depicting the Siboney Indians of Cuba. Oddly enough, Teok was one of my best friends in the Miami art scene, and before his death I talked with him.

"Hombre," said Teok, "how can I forget that time? Cesar was a very charming man but not very realistic. He had hired me to do several panels depicting the life of the Siboneys in Cuba. Well, you know they were killed off, by the Spaniards. Cesar didn't want to know that; he wanted pictures of the Spaniards and Indians in a friendly intercourse, smoking together and such. Also he was unrealistic about time. He wanted everything done by yesterday. Well, you know about art. It takes time. No one can hurry it up. In the meanwhile I was having a great time in Tampa, and the food at the Columbia was superb. The paintings eventually got done, but at Carrasco time, not Cesar time. I'm very proud of them and hope they add to the dimension of the room. I can only say I had a wonderful time, and Cesar and Adela were gracious hosts."

When they opened the Siboney Room, only one mural was done, and there was no set stage. But Cesar was determined to open, and on December 31, 1956, open they did.

ADELA: *It was two years before we finally built a proper bandstand and stage. For two years we had a frantic Keystone Cops moment when it came time to open a show. Tables were pushed aside at one end of the room, and carpenters would rush in and assemble a prefab foundation for a stage; then they would lay the stage on top of it, and the show would begin. It was awful. Embarrassing.*

The problem was that we had built the back wall flush with the back of the adjoining building so we were trapped in a limited space. The only solution was to buy the adjacent building and break through the wall. The obstacle proved to be my dad. With business falling off, he could not see investing further.

It remained for my mother to come to the rescue. She never interfered with business, but, just this once, she felt she had to. She had her own money in the bank, and she promptly gave us the funds to buy the building.

With the acquisition of the building, we built a great stage and bandstand. Now we could invite the great performing artists and not feel embarrassed.

F E R D I E : Their opening act was the famous Cuban pianist-composer Ernesto Lecuona. Adela was one of the leading interpreters of his music in the concert world, so she was in heaven. Lecuona, with his quiet dignity and beautiful music, was a big hit, and he packed them in for three months.

A D E L A : *I studied piano from the time I was small to when I was fourteen with Ferdie's step-grandmother, Pennsylvania Pacheco. At fourteen, I remember, I played Ernesto Lecuona's "Danza Lucumi" for her and she told me she had nothing further to teach me. I was the youngest person in Tampa certified to teach piano. My favorite composer then, as now, was Lecuona, so when I had the opportunity to engage him for the Siboney I jumped at the chance.*

F E R D I E : The room flourished as they booked the top Latin talent. Popular acts of the supper club circuit included Las Hermanas Marquez, Los Tres Galanes, and the talented Noro Morales.

The audience particularly favored flamenco, so Cesar booked the top dancers, singers, and entertainers, most of whom also had a big Anglo following. The most prestigious was the legendary Carmen Amaya, the fiery dancer who brought Sabicas, the best flamenco guitarist, with her. American audiences were familiar with José Greco, a Brooklyn-born Italian-Spanish dancer who had appeared on the cover of *Life* magazine and was at the top of his form in the concert circuit. He performed for three seasons at the Columbia.

As great a dancer as José Greco was, one of his former dancers, José Molina, who had acquired a following by appearing many times on Johnny

Carmen Amaya, the greatest female Spanish flamenco of all time, 1956. She was pure fire and soul.

José Molina, shown here in 1960, danced in Greco's troupe, then became a star performer through his many appearances on Johnny Carson's show. Some critics felt that he was the best Spanish dancer at the time. Photo by Ken Duncan.

Carson's *Tonight Show,* was Greco's superior. He was funny on the show but was dead serious on the Siboney stage. Adela rated him among the top dancers she had seen. He stayed for two seasons.

The classiest act to come out of Spain was an orchestra known as Los Chavales de España (Los Chavales means "The Kids"). They were as balanced an act as anyone has reason to expect. A tall, exceedingly handsome singer, Luis Tamayo, was a showstopper, and they always hired the best flamenco dancers available. My wife, Luisita Sevilla, danced with them for seven years before I took her away and booked her in my house for a lifetime run.

Local entertainers also added to the popularity of the room. Of these the two best were comic Jack Espinosa and singer Dalia Fernandez. Jack had spectacular success in Havana TV and faced a bright future, but he opted to stay in Tampa. Dalia was a popular favorite, but she too decided to stay at home and married a local architect, John Rañon, whose father, Domingo, had built the Siboney Room.

ADELA: *We found major talent and brought them to the Siboney. One of the best singer-entertainers, if not the best, I brought from New York, and she ended up staying fifteen years as part of our Siboney family.*

During a visit to New York I went to meet an old friend at the Chateau Madrid, one of the best nightclubs in Manhattan. There I saw Amparo Garrido for the first time. I was struck by her beauty, her stage presence, her voice, and by

Los Chavales de España with dancer Trini Reyes, 1955. The classiest act ever to interpret Spanish music. Every one of them was a versatile musician capable of playing several instruments well.

Amparo Garrido in 1968.
This beautiful Spanish
singer came, caused a
sensation, and stayed for
fifteen years.

*how she captivated the audience. I rushed back to the hotel to call Cesar. We had
to have her. She came to the Siboney, wowed the public, and stayed.*

*During these years we formed a sort of Siboney Troupe with Cesar, his orches-
tra, Garrido, and a good tenor, Antonio Curbelo, and also developed a Columbia
Flamenco Dance Troupe. I had a longstanding admiration for José Greco. When
I was at Juilliard I went to see him at the old Met in concert. He danced to
Rimsky-Korsakov's "Capriccio Español." I was swept off my feet. Never did I
think I'd ever be in a position to hire him to perform for us, and it was a big
thrill when we did.*

*The Columbia had been attracting celebrities since the 1930s. Athletes were
special customers. The New York Yankees trained in St. Petersburg, so everyone
expected to see their major stars at the Columbia. In that era they had the same
public impact as rock stars do today.*

*One of my earliest childhood memories was meeting Babe Ruth and Lou
Gehrig. I'd never imagined Ruth was so big. Another time my father came home
in midafternoon to dress me up and rush to the Columbia. There, eating his*

José Greco, the renowned Spanish dancer, visited the Columbia in 1949.
Left to right: Adela, Greco and friend, Cesar.

lunch at the Fonda, was Jack Dempsey, former heavyweight champion of the
world. He gave me a small set of gold-plated gloves with his initials on them.
We were so careless about photographers back then, and now I wonder why.

President John Kennedy at the Columbia. Cesar (far right) had a hard time getting close to JFK. This photo was taken in November 1963, days before Kennedy's assassination.

When Cesar took over, he was much more aware of publicity than my dad, and we had a photographer on call when a celebrity came to dine.

One I remember particularly was Jack Kennedy, who was running for reelection when he came to the restaurant. He had his full retinue with him, plus a crush of admirers around him. It was so bad that even Cesar didn't get next to him when our publicity picture was taken. Cesar isn't close, but he is smiling his beautiful smile.

Probably the reason that day stands out is that I was remembering the evenings in Washington, D.C., when Cesar was playing an engagement at the Mayflower Hotel and how almost every night Jack Kennedy was there, dancing with a dark-haired, slim beauty named Jacqueline Bouvier.

Among the celebrities who came, many enchanted us with their personalities.

Esther Williams was tall and shapely and had a gorgeous smile and down-to-earth personality. It didn't take her long to leap onstage and dance a mean rhumba with one of our dancers. Another one was Ricardo Montalban, her co-star in a movie they were making near Tampa. He was Hispanic and full of charm, heavenly handsome and **muy macho.**

Esther Williams got carried away by the rhumba beat and burst into dance with a band member, 1959. Cesar looked on with envy.

Another Hispanic movie star who lasted longer than most was Cesar Romero, who was the grandson of José Martí, the great nineteenth-century Cuban patriot. He had survived in Hollywood since the 1930s and was still working in the 1960s. He had a mane of silver hair and a California tan and was a genteel and cultured man.

Jack Espinosa, reminiscing with me recently, recalled another visitor: "We were about to go on one night when Cesar came backstage all excited and told us that Gary Moore and his new comic find, Carol Burnett, who was about twenty-

Two Cesars and a queen, 1959. Perennial movie star Cesar Romero (center) with Denise Martinez and Cesar Gonzmart, king and queen of the Krewe of Sant' Yago at Gasparilla, the annual Tampa festival celebrating the adventures of pirate José Gaspar.

Carol Burnett is overwhelmed by the continental charm of the hand-kissing Cesar Gonzmart, 1959.

five at the time, were out front. He told us how much this meant to us. It's all we needed to hear. We were dying.

"I was first up, and I mumbled a weak disclaimer to start. 'We've been told some very important TV personalities are in the audience and to do our best to impress them . . . so here goes.'

"I was doing a comedy record pantomime, and I gave it everything I had. After two records, Carol Burnett stood up and yelled, 'I'm impressed, I'm impressed! Stop before you kill yourself!'

"Then she hopped onstage, and we did about half an hour of impromptu comedy. It was wacky. It was wonderful."

Ferdie: In addition to movie, theatrical, and musical stars, athletes kept dropping in.

The boxer Two-Ton Galento impressed the entire kitchen staff when he set a Columbia record by dispatching seven plates of chicken and yellow rice. Two-Ton had come close to knocking out Joe Louis for the heavyweight championship but had failed. I guess he was eating to forget.

The biggest man I have ever seen dine at the Columbia was heavyweight champ Primo Carnera. As tall as Carnera was, Rocky Marciano was short. It was as if talent existed in inverse proportion to size. The huge guy was one of the worst heavyweights in the history of boxing, and Rocky, the short one, was one of the best, retiring undefeated. Rocky brought another Hall of Fame fighter with him to taste the delights of the Columbia. Willy Pep was called the Will o' Wisp for his expert defense. As usual, the little skinny Willy Pep out-ate the Brocton Blockbuster, Rocky Marciano.

We could fill the book with famous athletes who enjoyed the Columbia, but my personal drop-jaw stars were Joltin' Joe DiMaggio and the Splendid Splinter, Ted Williams. Both men in their prime were great physical specimens and handsome as movie stars.

✌ When the Spanish Civil War was raging in 1936, all the Tampa Spaniards sided with the Loyalists, the legitimate elected Republican government.

Adela: *I remember one day in 1934 the schools were let out so we could march in what was called a May Day parade. I was so happy to be free of school, to march with my classmates, holding hands, singing "Bandera Roja" ("Red*

Primo Carnera, former heavyweight champ, at the Columbia with Adela and Cesar in 1949. The largest heavyweight champ was not the best . . .

. . . but the smallest heavyweight champ was. The Brocton Blockbuster, Rocky Marciano, with Cesar in 1949.

Flag") and the "Internationale." We marched to the city hall where the lector, Victor Manteiga, made a rousing speech, and Mayor Chancey made a similar speech in English.

Boy, did I get it when I got home. My father was livid. It was his daughter marching in a Red parade, singing Communist songs. The shame of it. I was bewildered because I didn't know the difference between Reds and Franco's Fascists.

FERDIE: My grandfather Gustavo Jimenez was the consul from Spain and our house was the main headquarters for the Loyalist government. In our house the name Franco was hated in the same way Sherman was detested in southern homes.

The civil war in Spain ended in 1939, and soon we were involved in a much bigger conflict, World War II. Franco chose to sit that war out and passed from everyone's mind.

By 1965 Franco was seen as a benevolent dictator who pulled Spain out of her postwar misery and poverty and established order. His conservative, church-backed reforms brought Spain back into acceptance by the other nations. There was no crime, no pornography, none of the violence of the rest of the Western world.

It was in this climate of wary acceptance that Tampeños started to visit Spain in droves. Prices were cheap, and the dollar was king.

In 1965 the Columbia Restaurant entertained a special envoy to the New World, and he was so enthralled by what he saw and ate at the Columbia that he said he would include it in his report to Franco. The minister of tourism, Fraga Irribarne, must have turned in a superlative report, for soon Cesar and Adela were invited to visit Spain and meet the generalissimo.

Instructions from the government came after they arrived in Spain. Adela was to dress in a high-necked formal suit, gloves, and hat. Cesar was to dress in a cutaway coat and striped pants. He did hit one snag. Cesar was very tall and the average Spaniard very short, so he could not find a shirt with long enough sleeves. He had to have one made to order.

ADELA: *We were met by a man who looked like he came from central casting for a zarzuela. He was full of formal do's and don't's and almost danced as he talked and led us into a formal dining room. He was stiff and formal, but not enough to refrain from flirting with me. I pointed to Cesar, and with irrefutable*

Left to right: José Manuel (protocol aide), Adela, Cesar, and Generalissimo Francisco Franco, 1965. Cesar advises Franco on how to take care of the piled-up paperwork on his desk.

logic I said, "If I'm married to that gorgeous man, what would I need with you?"

Armed with boxes of Tampa cigars, a key to the city, and a streetcar transfer to the Sulphur Springs streetcar, we made our nervous entrance.

General Franco rose to meet us. The first thing I thought was that he was so small, old, and frail. His voice was low but very gentle and gracious. He was highly complimentary about the Columbia, and that set Cesar talking for about ten minutes. The general listened courteously; then he turned to me and said, "Tell me about you, your house, your children. Forget the formality, address me as General." Up to this point we had been advised to call him "Su Excelencia" (Your Excellency).

*As I was winding down I could not help but notice his desk, piled high with papers. "Ah, General, I see by your desk you have the same work habits as my grandfather and father, everything for **mañana.**"*

He laughed delightedly. He was having a good time. I had noticed that he had

*only allowed the representative of **Time-Life** a ten-minute audience. We had*
been there for thirty minutes, and Señor José Manuel, the flirtatious aide, was
running out of time. We made a gracious exit.

FERDIE: There was one thing they brought back to the Columbia from
their trip. General Franco had recommended that they eat at Horcher's Restaurant in Madrid. When Cesar took Adela there, they were amazed when a
waiter put a satin cushion under Adela's feet. This was a touch of originality
that appealed to the romantic Cesar. When they returned to Tampa, he insti-
tuted the service of satin foot cushions for ladies dining at the Columbia. It
lasted for two years.

DESSERTS ✿ POSTRES

Almond Cakes

Bizcochos de Almendras

1 cup butter

1 cup sugar

1 egg, separated

½ cup almond paste (do not use almond filling)

2 cups all-purpose flour, sifted

¼ cup flaked coconut (sweetened or unsweetened)

1 teaspoon almond extract

½ teaspoon baking powder

¼ cup sliced almonds

With electric mixer, beat butter and sugar until light and fluffy. Beat in egg yolk; reserve white for topping. Beat in almond paste and extract. Blend in flour, baking powder, and coconut. Press into ungreased 8-x-8-inch pan. Beat egg white until frothy; brush over top of dough. Cover evenly with almonds. Bake 30 minutes at 350° or until golden. Cut in squares. Makes about 16 squares.

Blueberry Pie

Pastel de Arándano Azul

4 cups blueberries, washed and picked over to remove foreign particles

1¼ cups sugar

2 tablespoons flour

2 tablespoons cornstarch

8 ounces cream cheese, softened

2 large eggs

½ cup heavy cream

1 teaspoon vanilla extract

Pastry for 1-crust 9-inch pie

Whipped cream for garnish, if desired

Roll out pastry dough ¼ inch thick on a floured surface, fit it into a 9-inch pie plate, and crimp edges decoratively. In a bowl combine blueberries, flour, cornstarch, and 1 cup of the sugar. With a fork, mash some of the berries to make juice. Stir blueberry mixture until sugar, flour, and cornstarch are dissolved in juice. Spoon mixture into pie shell and bake in lower third of a preheated 450° oven for 20 minutes. Remove from oven. Reduce heat to 350°.

In a bowl, beat together cream cheese, the remaining ¼ cup sugar, eggs, vanilla extract, and heavy cream until mixture is smooth. Pour mixture over pie; bake on middle rack at 350° for 45 minutes. Cool. Garnish with whipped cream if desired.

Bread Pudding

Pudín de Pan

1 loaf Cuban bread	*1 cup raisins*
¼ lb. butter or margarine, cut into small pieces	*1 cup almonds, skinned and chopped*
3 large eggs	*1 5-oz. can evaporated milk*
½ teaspoon salt	*2 cups sugar*
2 teaspoons vanilla extract	*1 cup guava paste, cut in small pieces*
2 teaspoons almond extract	
2 or 3 large apples, peeled and cut into small pieces	*Pineapple slices, maraschino cherries, and sliced almonds for garnish*
1 16-oz. can fruit cocktail, drained	

Cut bread into slices about 3 inches thick and soak them in water for 10 to 15 minutes to soften. Squeeze water out of bread, then place in colander for a few minutes to continue draining. Break bread in small pieces into a large mixing bowl.

Add all remaining ingredients except garnishes. Mix well and turn into large, buttered baking pan, about 9 x 13 inches. Bake at 350° for 1½ to 2 hours, or until a toothpick inserted in center comes out clean. For last 20 minutes of baking, decorate with pineapple slices, cherries, and almonds, if desired. The guava paste gives this bread pudding a distinctive flavor. Serves 8–10.

Caribbean Pineapple Cake

Bizcocho de Piña Caribeña

1 20-oz. can crushed pineapple
   in syrup
2 cups Bisquick baking mix
1 cup all-purpose flour, sifted
1 teaspoon baking soda

1 cup sugar
¾ cup sour cream
½ cup margarine or butter, softened
2 teaspoons vanilla extract
2 large eggs

Drain pineapple well, saving syrup for glaze. Combine baking mix, flour, and soda. In a separate bowl, beat eggs, sugar, sour cream, margarine, and vanilla extract together for 2 minutes. Add flour mixture and beat 1 minute longer. Mix in drained pineapple. Turn into well-greased 9-inch bundt pan. Bake at 350° about 45 minutes, or until toothpick inserted in middle comes out clean. (While cake is baking, make glaze; see below.) Remove cake from oven and spoon about half the glaze evenly over it. Let stand 10 minutes; turn out onto serving plate and spoon on remaining glaze. Cool before cutting.

GLAZE
¾ cup sugar
¼ cup margarine or butter

¼ cup syrup from pineapple
2 tablespoons rum (optional)

Combine sugar, margarine, and pineapple syrup. Stir over low heat until sugar is dissolved and butter is melted. Remove from heat and stir in rum.

Chocolate Cake

Bizcocho de Chocolate

3 1-oz. blocks unsweetened
   chocolate, melted
1 cup boiling water
1¼ teaspoons baking soda
½ cup butter, softened
1 teaspoon vanilla extract

2 cups sugar
3 eggs, separated
2½ cups cake flour, sifted
½ teaspoon salt
1 cup sour cream

Combine chocolate and water, cool slightly, and add soda. In a separate bowl, cream butter and 1½ cups sugar. Add egg yolks and beat well. In another bowl, sift flour and salt together. Add flour mixture to egg mixture alternately with sour cream, beating after each addition until smooth. Add chocolate mixture and vanilla extract.

In another bowl, beat egg whites until soft peaks form; add remaining sugar. Fold into batter. Pour into 2 9-inch cake pans lined with waxed paper. Bake at 350° 40 to 45 minutes. Cool on wire racks for 10 minutes before removing cake from pans. Frost with chocolate icing after cake has cooled.

CHOCOLATE ICING
5 1-oz. blocks unsweetened
   chocolate
2 cups sifted confectioners' sugar
6 tablespoons butter, softened

6 tablespoons milk
¼ teaspoon salt
1 teaspoon vanilla extract
1 egg

Melt chocolate over boiling water and cool slightly. Add rest of ingredients and beat with electric mixer. Set bowl over larger bowl containing ice cubes and beat mixture until it reaches spreading consistency.

Chocolate Mousse Cake

❧

Bizcocho de Mousse de Chocolate

MOUSSE

1 tablespoon unflavored gelatin
¼ cup cold water
⅔ cup sugar
¼ teaspoon salt
1¾ cups milk

3 eggs, separated
1 4-oz. package sweet baking
    chocolate
1 teaspoon vanilla extract

Soften gelatin in ¼ cup cold water. Set aside. Combine milk, salt, and ⅓ cup of the sugar in medium saucepan. Add chocolate. Cook over medium heat, stirring constantly, until chocolate is completely melted. Blend well with egg beater. Add small amount of hot mixture to 3 lightly beaten egg yolks, stirring vigorously. Gradually add remaining hot mixture, stirring constantly. Return to saucepan and cook over low heat until mixture is slightly thickened, about 5 minutes. Remove from heat.

Add softened gelatin and stir until dissolved. Pour into large bowl and chill until partially thickened. Stir in vanilla extract. Beat 3 egg whites until foamy. Add remaining ⅓ cup sugar to egg whites, 2 tablespoons at a time; continue beating just until stiff peaks form. Fold into chilled chocolate mixture. Spoon into a 1½-quart mixing bowl and chill until firm, about 2½ hours.

CAKE

3 1-oz. blocks unsweetened
    chocolate, melted
½ cup butter, softened
1 teaspoon vanilla extract
2 cups sugar
2½ cups all-purpose flour, sifted
1 cup boiling water
1¼ teaspoons baking soda

1 cup sour cream
½ teaspoon red food coloring
3 eggs, separated
½ teaspoon salt
Chocolate curls for garnish
    (optional)
1 cup whipping cream (for
    frosting)

Combine chocolate and boiling water. Cool slightly. Add baking soda. In separate bowl, cream butter and 1½ cups of sugar; add egg yolks and vanilla; beat well. In another bowl, sift flour and salt together. Add flour mixture to egg mixture alternately with sour cream, beating after each addition until smooth. Add chocolate mixture and food coloring. Beat egg whites until soft peaks form and add remaining ½ cup of sugar; fold into batter. Pour into 2 9-inch cake pans lined with waxed paper. Bake at 350° 40 to 45 minutes. Cool. Remove from pans and place 1 layer on cake plate. (Freeze other layer for future use.)

Whip 1 cup whipping cream until stiff peaks form. When cake is completely cool, loosen chocolate mousse mold at top edge with a sharp knife. Place in bowl of warm water for a few seconds. Remove from water and shake bowl gently to loosen. Invert cake over bowl and flip over so that mousse is atop cake. Spread whipped cream over mousse cake. The finished cake will be in the shape of the bowl and will look like a baked Alaska. Garnish with chocolate curls, if desired. Keep refrigerated before serving.

Chocolate Whipped-Cream Roll

Brazo de Gitano de Chocolate

FILLING

3 egg yolks

¾ cups sugar

½ cup unsweetened cocoa

3 cups milk

⅛ teaspoon salt

3 tablespoons cornstarch

2 teaspoons vanilla extract

In medium-size, heavy-bottomed saucepan, beat egg yolks until lemon-colored. Add sugar and beat well. Dissolve cornstarch in a little of the milk and add to mixture. Add cocoa, salt, and remainder of milk. Cook over medium heat, stirring constantly with a wire whisk, until mixture thickens and boils. Boil, still stirring, for 1 minute. Remove from heat and stir in vanilla extract. Cool.

Cake

7 eggs, separated	*3 tablespoons cake flour*
7 tablespoons sugar	*4 tablespoons unsweetened cocoa*

Sift flour and cocoa together. Beat egg whites and sugar with electric mixer until stiff; add egg yolks gradually. Lower speed, add flour-cocoa mixture, and blend well. Pour into waxed-paper-lined jelly roll pan (11 x 16 x 1 inch size). Bake at 400° for 8 to 10 minutes. Sprinkle a cloth kitchen towel with sugar. When cake is done, immediately invert onto towel. Remove waxed paper. Spread cake with chocolate filling and roll up lengthwise like a jelly roll. Place on serving dish and pour syrup (see below) over cake. Cool and frost with icing (see below). To serve, cut crosswise as you would cut a jelly roll.

Syrup

1 cup sugar
1 cup water
½ cup coffee or chocolate liqueur

Boil sugar and water until sugar dissolves; add liqueur.

Icing

5 squares unsweetened chocolate, melted	*1 egg*
	½ cup milk
3 cups sifted confectioners' sugar, sifted	*6 tablespoons butter, softened*
	2 teaspoons vanilla extract

Combine all ingredients in mixing bowl. Set bowl in a larger bowl containing ice cubes and beat mixture until it reaches spreading consistency.

Coconut Cream Pie

Pastel de Coco y Crema

1 9-inch pie crust, baked	3 cups milk
3 egg yolks	1 tablespoon butter
½ cup sugar	2 teaspoons vanilla extract
½ teaspoon salt	1 cup grated coconut (frozen
½ cup cornstarch	unsweetened or fresh)

In heavy saucepan beat yolks until lemon-colored. Beat in sugar and salt. Dissolve cornstarch in a little of the milk. Add to yolk mixture with rest of milk. Cook over medium heat, stirring constantly, until thickened. Remove from heat. Add butter, vanilla extract, and ¾ cup coconut; mix well. Cool and pour into pie shell. Spread meringue (see below) over custard; sprinkle with ¼ cup coconut. Return to oven for 5 minutes at 400° or until lightly browned.

MERINGUE
3 egg whites
6 tablespoons sugar
¼ teaspoon cream of tartar

Beat egg whites with cream of tartar until stiff peaks form. Add sugar very gradually until smooth.

Congo Squares

Cuadritos de Congo

2 sticks margarine
1 16-oz. package brown sugar
3 large eggs
2½ cups all-purpose flour
2 teaspoons baking soda

¼ teaspoon salt
1 teaspoon vanilla extract
1 6-oz. package chocolate chips
1 cup pecans, chopped

   Melt sugar and margarine together. Cool. Add eggs; beat well. Sift together flour, soda, and salt. Mix well. Add pecans, vanilla extract, and chocolate. Spread in greased 13 x 9-inch pan. Bake at 350° for 25 to 30 minutes. Cool and cut into squares (makes about 20).

Cream Catalana

Crema Catalana

4 egg yolks
½ cup sugar
¼ cup cornstarch
2 cups milk
1 strip of lemon peel

1 strip of orange peel
1 cinnamon stick
½ teaspoon salt
1 tablespoon vanilla extract

   Beat egg yolks lightly in stainless steel or any nonstick saucepan. Add sugar; beat well with wire whisk. Add cornstarch and milk; mix thoroughly. Add salt, lemon peel, orange peel, and cinnamon stick. Blend well and cook over medium heat, stirring constantly. When custard thickens, cool for one minute, stirring. Remove from heat, add vanilla extract, remove cinnamon stick and lemon and orange peel, and cool (in individual ovenproof ramekins or ovenproof serving dish). Sprinkle with sugar and place directly under broiler until sugar caramelizes. Serves 4–6.

Cream-Filled Roll

Brazo de Gitano

FILLING

5 egg yolks (reserve whites for
   meringue)
2 cups milk
⅓ cup cornstarch

½ cup sugar
1 cinnamon stick
1 teaspoon vanilla extract
Pinch salt

In heavy saucepan, beat egg yolks with wooden spoon until lemon-colored. Add sugar and salt; beat well. Dissolve cornstarch in a little of the milk; add with rest of milk to egg mixture. Add cinnamon stick. Cook over medium heat, stirring constantly, till mixture thickens to a heavy custard. Remove from heat, add vanilla extract, and remove cinnamon stick. Set aside to cool.

CAKE

7 eggs, separated
¾ cup sugar
1 cup cake flour, sifted

Beat egg whites in electric mixer at high speed until soft peaks form. Add yolks, one at a time. Add sugar, 1 tablespoon at a time. Lower speed of mixer to folding speed and add flour gradually. Bake in wax-paper-lined jelly roll pan (11 x 16 x 1 inch size) at 400° for 12 minutes. Sprinkle cloth kitchen towel with sugar. When cake is done, immediately invert on towel. Remove waxed paper. Spread cake with filling and roll up lengthwise like a jelly roll. Place on an ovenproof serving tray. Soak cake slowly with syrup (see below). Cover completely with meringue (see below) and bake at 425° for 6–8 minutes or until meringue is lightly browned. To serve, cut cake crosswise as you would cut a jelly roll.

SYRUP

1½ cups sugar	½ cup dry sherry
1 cup water	1 strip of lemon peel

Boil sugar, water, and lemon peel for about 10 minutes. Add sherry. Remove lemon peel.

MERINGUE

5 egg whites
¼ teaspoon cream of tartar
1 cup sugar

Combine egg whites and cream of tartar. Beat with electric mixer until soft peaks form. Start adding sugar very gradually and beat until stiff.

Guava Cheesecake

Torta de Guayaba y Queso

CRUST

1½ cups graham cracker crumbs
¼ cup sugar
1 stick melted butter

In medium bowl combine cracker crumbs, sugar, and butter. Press mixture into lightly greased 9-inch springform pan; cover bottom and ½ inch up the side. Bake for 6 minutes at 375°. Cool.

FILLING

32 ounces cream cheese, softened	*¼ cup all-purpose flour*
1¼ cups sugar	*¼ teaspoon salt*
5 large eggs	*2 16-oz. cans guava shells*

Drain guava shells, reserving syrup. Puree half of shells in a food processor, saving other half for topping. In large bowl or electric mixer, beat cream cheese until fluffy. Add sugar gradually. Add eggs one at a time, beating after each addition. Beat in remaining ingredients. Pour into crust. Bake in 325° preheated oven about 1 hour and 15 minutes. Turn oven off, open door slightly, and leave cake in oven for 30 minutes. Remove from oven. Cool. Arrange guava shells on top and cover cake with glaze (see below). Serve cold or at room temperature.

GLAZE

1 cup guava syrup
2 teaspoons cornstarch
2 tablespoons sugar

Blend syrup, cornstarch, and sugar. Cook over low heat, stirring constantly, until smooth and thick. Cool.

Italian Sesame Cookies

Galletas Italianas de Ajonjoli

2½ cups all-purpose flour
2 teaspoons baking powder
½ teaspoon salt
1 cup sugar
1½ teaspoons cinnamon

3 eggs, beaten
1 teaspoon vanilla extract
5 tablespoons solid shortening
2 lbs. sesame seeds

Sift first 5 ingredients together. Blend in shortening. Gradually add eggs and vanilla extract and knead into a ball. For each cookie, scoop out a heaping soup spoonful of dough and roll into the shape of a small cigar (3 to 4 inches long). Roll each cookie in sesame seeds, slightly dampened to make them stick. Bake at 350° for 25–30 minutes or until golden brown. Makes 3–4 dozen.

Melba's Cake

Bizcocho de Melba

1 box Jiffy yellow cake mix
1 20-oz. can crushed pineapple
   in its own juice
1 8-oz. package cream cheese

2 cups milk
1 3.4-oz. package vanilla instant
   pudding mix
1 9-oz. container whipped topping

Prepare cake mix as directed and bake in a 13 x 9 x 2-inch pan for 8 minutes only (cake will be thin). Invert cake onto serving platter. Pour pineapple over cake, juice and all. Mix cream cheese, pudding mix, and milk and allow to thicken. Spread over cake and pineapple. Spoon whipped topping over cake and refrigerate for 1 day before serving.

Peach Parfait Pie

❧

Pastel de Melocotón Parfait

1 3-oz. package peach or lemon
   gelatin
1¼ cups hot water
1 pint peach or vanilla ice cream
¼ cup sugar

Pastry for 1-crust 9-inch pie, baked
½ cup heavy cream
1 cup fresh peaches, peeled and
   diced
Toasted sliced almonds for garnish

Dissolve gelatin in hot water. Immediately add ½ cup ice cream and stir until blended. Gradually stir in rest of ice cream. Chill until almost firm. Mix peaches with sugar and fold into mixture. Pour into cooled pie shell and chill until firm. Whip cream until peaks form; spread on pie. Sprinkle with almonds.

PASTRY FOR ONE-CRUST PIE

1 cup all-purpose flour
½ teaspoon salt
6 tablespoons margarine or solid
shortening (such as Crisco)

3½ tablespoons iced water

Mix flour and salt. Add margarine and shortening; mix with a fork or pastry blender until mixture resembles coarse cornmeal. Add water 1 tablespoon at a time, tossing lightly until dough leaves the side of the bowl. Shape into a ball, wrap in waxed paper, and refrigerate for 30 minutes. On pastry cloth or board, roll into a circle to fit into 9-inch pie pan; trim edges. Prick bottom or weight down (for example, with dried beans on waxed paper) to prevent air bubbles. Bake at 425° for about 10 minutes or until lightly browned.

Powdered Cookies

Galletas Polvorones

1 cup vegetable shortening	½ teaspoon baking powder
1 cup plus 2 tablespoons sugar	¼ teaspoon salt
2 eggs	1 tablespoon Spanish brandy
4 cups all-purpose flour	Confectioners' sugar

Cream shortening, sugar, and eggs (1 at a time) in large bowl. Sift flour, baking powder, and salt; add to egg mixture. Add brandy and mix well. Dough should be smooth and compact. Roll out on pastry cloth until dough is ½ inch thick. Cut with round cookie cutter about 1 inch in diameter. Bake on lightly greased cookie sheet at 375° until lightly browned (12–15 minutes). Cool. Dust with confectioners' sugar. Makes about 48 cookies.

Rice Pudding

Arroz con Leche

½ cup short-grained rice, uncooked	4 cups milk
	1 cinnamon stick
½ teaspoon salt	1 cup sugar
2 strips lemon peel	Ground cinnamon
1½ cups water	

Combine rice, water, salt, and lemon peel; bring to a boil. Cook over low heat until rice is done (about 18 minutes). Remove lemon peel. In a heavy-bottomed saucepan, scald milk (heat until bubbles form at edge), with cinnamon stick. Add milk and cinnamon stick to cooked rice and cook over low heat, stirring often with wooden spoon. When mixture is creamy, add sugar and continue cooking and stirring for approximately 5 minutes. Remove from heat; remove cinnamon stick. Pudding should be creamy and not too thick; it will thicken as it cools. When ready to serve, sprinkle with ground cinnamon. Serves 6.

Spanish Custard

Flan

6 tablespoons sugar	1 cinnamon stick
6 eggs	2 cups milk
1 teaspoon vanilla extract	Pinch salt
1 strip lemon peel	Caramelized sugar (see below)

CUSTARD

Boil milk with lemon peel and cinnamon stick. Lightly beat eggs with wire whisk. Blend in sugar, vanilla extract, and salt. Add milk gradually; strain. Pour into ovenproof custard cups with caramelized sugar in bottoms (see below). Place cups in pan of hot water (2 inches deep) and bake in oven for 1 hour at 300°. Never let water boil or custard will be filled with holes. Remove from pan and cool in refrigerator. To serve, unmold by pressing edges of custard with spoon to break away from cup, then turning upside down. Spoon caramelized sugar from bottoms of cups over top of each custard. Makes 6 small servings.

CARAMELIZED SUGAR

1 cup sugar
1 tablespoon water

Place sugar and water in small skillet. Cook over medium heat, stirring constantly, until sugar is golden. Pour immediately into 6 ovenproof custard cups.

Spanish French Toast

Torrijas

1 loaf Cuban or French bread
4 cups milk
3 ounces dry Spanish sherry
Cinnamon

3 eggs
Vegetable oil for frying
Sherry syrup (see below)

Cut bread in 1-inch slices; trim edges. Soak bread in milk. Drain, sprinkle with wine, and dust with cinnamon. Beat eggs until slightly foamy. Dip bread slices in egg and drain. Fry bread in hot oil (½ inch deep in skillet) until golden. Drain and place on serving platter. Soak in sherry syrup.

SHERRY SYRUP
½ cup water
1½ cups sugar

1 strip of lemon peel
¼ cup Spanish cream sherry

Boil water, sugar, and lemon peel until sugar is well dissolved. Remove from heat and add wine.

Spice Cake

❧

Bizcocho de Especias

2¼ cups cake flour

1 teaspoon baking powder

¾ teaspoon baking soda

½ teaspoon salt

¾ teaspoon ground cloves

¾ teaspoon cinnamon

Pinch pepper

¾ cup butter or margarine, softened

¾ cup brown sugar, firmly packed

1 cup white sugar

1 teaspoon vanilla extract

3 eggs

1 cup buttermilk or sour milk

Preheat oven to 350°. Grease and flour bottoms and sides of 2 9-inch cake pans. Sift cake flour, measure, and sift again with baking powder, soda, spices, and salt. Cream butter; add brown sugar, beating well. Add white sugar; blend well. Add eggs 1 at a time, beating well after each addition. Add flour mixture and milk alternately, mixing at low speed. Add vanilla extract and blend. Pour batter into prepared pans and bake 30 to 35 minutes. Remove from oven. Cool for 5 minutes and turn out onto a cake rack; cool thoroughly. Frost with sea foam frosting (see below).

SEA FOAM FROSTING (*MERENGUE ESPECIAL*)

2 egg whites

1½ cups dark brown sugar,
  firmly packed

⅓ cup water

1 teaspoon vanilla extract

Beat all ingredients except vanilla extract at high speed in top of double boiler over boiling water for 4 minutes. Add vanilla extract. Remove from hot water. Beat one more minute. Spread evenly on cake.

Walnut-Filled Turnovers

※

Casadielles (Bollinas)

Frozen puff pastry or pie dough
  (see p. 248)
1 cup ground walnuts
½ cup sugar
½ teaspoon cinnamon

1 tablespoon sherry
1 tablespoon melted butter
1 egg, lightly beaten, for glazing
Granulated sugar

Follow frozen puff pastry instructions or prepare pastry. Mix nuts, sugar, and cinnamon. Stir in sherry and butter. Roll pastry to ⅛ inch. Cut into 3½-inch circles. Fill each circle with 1 tablespoon walnut filling. Brush edges with water, fold over, and press with a fork to seal well. Brush with beaten egg. Bake in 400° oven for about 10 minutes. Sprinkle with sugar. Serve warm or at room temperature. Makes 12–14 turnovers.

*Note: Many of the Spaniards who immigrated to Tampa in the early part of the twentieth century came from the province of Asturias in northern Spain. Even though this delicious dessert is called **casadielles** in most of Asturias, the immigrants from one remote section of the province called them **bollinas**.*

Yellow Cake

※

Bizcocho Amarillo

2 sticks butter

2 cups sugar

4 eggs

1 teaspoon vanilla extract

3 cups self-rising flour

1 cup milk (at room temperature)

In large mixing bowl, cream butter and sugar for 10 minutes at medium speed. Add eggs 1 at a time, beating well after each addition. Lower speed. Add flour gradually, alternating with milk. When all is blended, add vanilla extract. Pour into two well-greased 9-inch cake pans and bake in middle of oven at 350° for 25 minutes. Cool on racks for 10 minutes; then invert and remove from pan. Cool before icing with Seven-Minute Icing.

Seven-Minute Icing

2 egg whites (¼ cup)

1½ cups sugar

¼ teaspoon cream of tartar (or 1
   tablespoon light corn syrup)

⅓ cup water

1 teaspoon vanilla extract

Combine egg whites, sugar, cream of tartar, and water in top of double boiler. Beat at high speed for 1 minute with electric hand mixer. Place over boiling water (water should not touch bottom of pan); beat at high speed for 7 minutes. Remove pan from stove and add vanilla. Beat 2 minutes more at high speed. Frosts two 8- or 9-inch layers or a 13 x 9-inch cake.

Chapter Ten

CHILDREN

ADELA: *Our children, Casey and Richard, have proved to be a blessing and have repaid all the time and love we invested in them many times over. They are two splendid young men who are following in our footsteps. They are good family men, excellent businessmen, involved in the business and in the community. Our heritage, to put back into the community as we have received from it, continues in their lives.*

One incident crystallized in my mind how our children were coping with our overindulgences. After all, there is a trap connected with trying to give your children everything you can afford. They get spoiled. That was our constant worry.

When both were at Jesuit High School, I had a chance to talk to one of the top priests in charge of students, Father Lashley. At that time I felt we might have exceeded the boundaries of indulgence. Richard at sixteen had gotten a Pontiac Trans-Am. Casey at fifteen had received a Ford Thunderbird convertible.

"The best thing about your boys is that they keep their feet on the ground. They want to be part of the student body, not above it. They almost hid these cars before anyone saw them. They handle themselves very well. You should be proud."

Well, I was proud, and still am proud about how they conduct themselves.

One thing we tried to do was be totally impartial. Everything had to be fifty-fifty. If we gave Richard something, we gave Casey an equivalent thing. We never favored one over the other. In that way I believe we brought up boys who got along well and were never envious of each other.

FERDIE: Casey is a darkly handsome, hefty six-foot-three and bears a passing resemblance to his Uncle Evelio. He was born in a trunk, the privileged show business baby. When he was four, the family gave up life on the road, settled back down in Tampa, and thereafter Casey grew up in the warm familiar confines of his grandfather Casimiro's house on Seventh Avenue in Tampa Heights.

"The first thing I can remember," says Casey, "is being in the kitchen watching my grandmother, Carmita, preparing the Sunday dinner, which was always the same. She marinated the chicken with lemon and garlic, and the potatoes were cooked in chicken broth. I can remember exactly the delicious aroma that came from the oven as she roasted the chicken and potatoes. She would let me do little tasks and from time to time taste things she was making. Then, at a certain hour, the entire family would sit down to eat, including my grandfather, Casimiro, who would never miss Sunday dinner, nor be late.

"Growing up in that house was like growing up in Havana or Madrid. I did not speak English when I started school at five. I was very happy being involved with Casimiro and my dad, hearing nothing but talk of the Columbia at my house.

"Unlike my brother, Richard, who was great in music and excelled in sports, I always had a one-track mind about myself, who I was, and where I was going. I cannot remember wanting to do anything but be involved in the Columbia Restaurant.

"I remember once waiting anxiously for my grandfather, Casimiro, to wake up so I could impart some exciting news to him. I sat with him as he had his *café con leche,* and he asked what I had discovered.

"Excitedly I said, 'I discovered a place with a great new chef. You have to hire him for the Columbia. He has invented something called a hamburger. They serve it on a bun with onions.'

"With a barely suppressed smile, my grandfather asked me if I had noted the place so that he could go and try the new dish himself.

"I told him it was called the Goody Goody, and another interesting facet he should look into was that if the customer was in a hurry he could have the food brought to his car and served on a tray that hooked on the window.

The Columbia family in 1965. The Gonzmarts are next to George (in chef's hat on left): Richard (today president of the Columbia Corporations), Cesar, Casey (today chairman of the board), and Adela, seated in front of them.

"He thanked me and said no more. To this day we don't serve hamburgers at the Columbia, but it's not because I didn't try to tell him.

"I was close to my mom and grandmother but saw my dad and Casimiro sparingly. During the summers we would take a house at the beach for a month, and they would come whenever they could wedge out the time. What I'm saying is that my dad did not have a great impact on my life as a child. All I heard while I was growing up was the importance of this place called the Columbia."

When he was deemed old enough, Casey was allowed to work at the Columbia, where, through a procession of endless summers, he learned every facet of the business, from the wine cellar to the sandwich board.

He was the youngest graduate from Jesuit High School at fifteen, and Adela and Cesar had a tough choice to make. Should they allow him to stay in Tampa, work at the restaurant, and grow a mite older, or send him to an Ivy League restaurant school, or let him begin at the top in Europe? Cesar opted for the top. They would send Casey, at sixteen years of age, to Europe. One can imagine Adela's heart skipping a beat. A kid who had grown up surrounded by adoring ladies, sheltered, pampered, and unprepared for street life, was to be sent to Paris at the age of sixteen to sink or swim. How would he feel?

Casey says, "I left Tampa and my identity was Casey of the Columbia, and when they dropped me off in Paris I became Casey the American. My parents and Richard went over on the SS *France* with me, and then we took a six-week tour of Europe. Finally they left me at the Alliance Française to learn French and got me a job at a great restaurant on the Champs Elysées called Ledoyen. I worked in the kitchen at night and went to school during the day.

"Did I experience culture shock? Actually, I had already lived through that feeling once before. When I went to preschool on Davis Island I did not speak a word of English, and I was from a European household, so I did not relate to the Anglo kids. If a teacher held up a green card, I said '*Verde,*' and she'd say, 'Green.' I was a veteran of culture shock. I was used to adapting.

"Of course, don't think I was a poor waif left alone to my resources, to make my way in the hostile atmosphere of Paris. Far from it. I had plenty of money, my own American Express card so I could eat in the fine restaurants, and I drove a brand new MGB sports car. I was sixteen, on my own, studying exactly what I wanted, and seeing nothing but good things on the horizon.

"Homesick? Yeah. I missed the warmth of my family, particularly their kindness and love, and their gaiety and fun. I missed the sea. The sun, white sand, and smell of salt water, the sound of the waves, the big red ball of the sun dropping into the Gulf. And I missed sports. Big-time. Of course, a sixteen-year-old is adaptable. In no time I was into soccer, and when I got to Spain I got hopelessly hooked on bullfights. They were very impressive to a young kid who was brought up in a restaurant decorated with tiles glorifying the corrida and the great Manolete.

"But when you are busy and have some francs to spend, and an MGB to visit the sea with, and new friends and new girlfriends, then somehow you overcome homesickness.

"Soon it was time to move on, and I went to Lausanne, Switzerland, to a great school named L'Ecole Hotelier. I was really in heaven there. I was still

Casey the American, but I had company. That school was a United Nations of cultures. We had twenty-four different nations represented in our classes. Then for the first time in my life, the outside world intruded on my happy life as a student. The Six-Day War started, and I saw the student body divide and take sides. Arabs and Jews who had been friends, who drank and partied together, were suddenly in punch-outs.

"My time to get involved came around when I had to register at the American consulate for the draft. Vietnam was still perking along, and now I could no longer ignore it. I registered and was given a number. The government had started the draft lottery, and my number never came up. Considering that I had grown up in Ybor City during the bolita days, I wasn't surprised."

By the time he moved on to a school in Spain, Casey had met up with an old stateside flame who later hit it big in Madrid as a model. Now his training slowed up as his social life escalated. It was to prove a dangerous curve in the road.

"The first thing that happened was good," says Casey. "I had all this Swiss money, and I had had no time to spend it, so when I got settled in Madrid I converted it to pesetas. By gosh, I was a millionaire! And things were so cheap in Madrid.

"Well, I lived the good life to the hilt. I was going out with this blonde goddess and her beautiful friends, and even in Spain the million didn't last long.

"The inevitable happened when my dad got wind of my high living, blonde goddess, and absences from school. I got into immediate hot sauce. When I wouldn't give up my goddess, Dad did an uncharacteristic thing: he cut me off. He was hardheaded, and so was I. As in a bad movie, I was down to my last peseta, and the goddess and I went into the street and bought a *chorizo* with our last change. We did not have an idea of how to pay for breakfast when Dad suddenly relented and sent a check. After all, Cesar Gonzmart was an incurable romantic. How could he, of all people, not understand a romance like mine?"

When Casey returned to Tampa, much had changed. Many of the old guard at the Columbia had died, and Ybor City was beginning to disintegrate. But the Columbia was still the bastion against decay.

Fortunately, Cesar was beginning to implement a long-range master plan.

He saw the day when Columbia Restaurants would spread across the state. His first venture would be in Sarasota, and naturally he turned to his firstborn son, now a graduate of the best restaurant schools in Europe, to take over the helm.

Casey had been home only a few months, and he was on the road again.

"I was twenty-one years old, the manager of the Sarasota Columbia, and I found out I had a new identity: I was Casey the European. It seemed to me that I was always the outsider, the sore thumb.

"I appeared at the restaurant in hand-tailored suits, with a continental haircut and a flashy car. Sarasota was a sleepy town in the middle of the state. You can guess what the people thought of me.

"I came for a few months and stayed for twenty years. I came to love it. I had no one over me, no one to veto my ideas, force theirs on me, and, in short, I was doing what I was trained for, to be the boss.

"I had learned about different cultures and people in Europe. I had to develop self-reliance. I had no one to turn to, not even peer friends, since I had always moved before I developed close friends. It made me insular, perhaps tough. I learned I could count on myself.

"In Sarasota I rounded out my education. I Americanized myself. I picked up my interest in sports. I went back to the beach. I became Casey the American again, and slowly I quit going back to Tampa for dental appointments and to buy clothes. More and more, I stayed in Sarasota. Finally, I found I had cut myself loose.

"The restaurant boomed as the growth of Sarasota exploded, while at home the old Columbia hung on, kept open by the tenacity and will power of my parents, and Ybor City imploded all around it.

"One thing I lacked was entertainment, and I could see how Dad was keeping the Columbia alive with entertainment. Without telling Dad anything, I decided to add a supper club. What could I have been thinking of? We were almost finished when I saw Dad's Rolls pull up to the front.

"Without a word he walked around and inspected what I was doing. He did not scold me, but I could see he was hurt. I had not consulted him. Still, he saw the idea was good, the construction solid, the cost reasonable, so he got back in his car and drove back to Tampa.

"Unlike my brother, Richard, I never worked under my dad. I felt free to do what I thought best. I built a highly successful operation which is today one of our best locations.

"Did I miss out on something? Well, yes and no. My dad let me get strong through independence. On the other hand, I loved him a great deal and would have liked to know him better. He was a great character, one of a kind, and had visionary dreams that are today coming true. We freeze and ship Columbia food—his idea. We have opened in thirteen locations and are doing well. His dream to expand is coming true. His guts held the old Columbia together. He saw Ybor City make a comeback, and in the middle of it all is the old flagship, the Columbia, Gem of All Spanish Restaurants."

Casey has a growing family, and he envisions the day they will all be involved in the family operation. His children—Lindsay, a thirteen-year-old girl, Casey, Jr., a ten-year-old, and eight-year-old Jessica—are all being groomed to be part of the continuing Columbia saga.

❦ Richard looks smaller than his six feet two inches, 220 pounds, indicate. He is compact and walks with an athlete's grace. His easygoing, friendly style masks a hardworking, ambitious man who still inflicts the discipline of the sports arena on himself.

By the time Richard came along, Cesar and Adela were happily ensconced in their Davis Island home.

Richard says, "It was a perfect childhood. My parents let me do anything within reason, and my mother encouraged me to bring my friends home. When I started applying myself seriously to football, our neighborhood team played on my front lawn. We really tore it up, but my parents never said a word."

As soon as he was old enough, Richard evinced a love of animal life. He started to collect many species, and he kept them in cages in front of his house on an empty lot that faced the bay.

At various times Richard had a hundred chickens, six quails, two turkeys, two iguanas, twenty-three cats, and a variety of dogs. He was a born farmer at heart.

Two events put an end to the Gonzmart Zoo. One year his chickens hatched a hundred chicks, 80 percent of which were roosters. The racket at 4:30 in the morning was incredible. Since they lived in an exclusive residential area, it did not take long to hear from their neighbors. One night Cesar, just settling in for a night's rest after a late night at the Columbia, was awakened by a phone call from his neighbor, Mr. Roberts.

"Cesar, I'd like to meet you outside of your house."

"Do you know what time it is, Mr. Roberts?"

"I certainly do, Cesar, it's 4:30 in the morning. That's what I want to talk to you about."

Sleepily, Cesar threw on his robe and went outside. He was met by a grim-faced Mr. Roberts and the din of eighty roosters proclaiming loudly the arrival of a new day.

"I can't hear you with all that noise," yelled Cesar.

"Exactly," said Mr. Roberts, satisfied that he had made his point.

The net result was a gigantic neighborhood barbecue, in which Adela and Cesar served up eighty roosters. Peace returned to Davis Island.

ADELA: *It was a splendid barbecue, but none of us could eat these chickens. To us it was like eating our family, so we smiled a lot but didn't touch the main meal.*

The other event that curtailed young Richard's ambitions was his announcement that he wanted to raise pigs. Even the softhearted Cesar balked at that. Richard's farmer days were over.

Cesar was no disciplinarian. I had a hard time convincing him that Richard had a fierce temper. Cesar just wouldn't believe it.

FERDIE: One day Cesar came home in the midst of one of Richard's worst temper tantrums. He was hitting the expensive dining table with a hammer. Faced with this extravagant display of out-of-control temper, Cesar was forced to discipline Richard.

"I was caught in mid-tantrum," says Richard. "Dad was going to spank me, and I calmed down and accepted it. I knew I was wrong. Well, he tried to spank me. After a few feeble, halfhearted swings, he gave up. I straightened up and volunteered to go to my room, and I was shocked to see him crying. He was a great dad, but couldn't stand to strike us. He never spanked me again."

"Growing up in a musician's house, I was torn between my love of sports and the familial talent in the music field. At six, I started taking piano but abandoned it after two years. (I still play a little, but barely.) Then I decided violin would be good and stuck with that for a while, but just getting a normal sound out of a violin is a hard task. By that time I wanted to follow athletics full-time. My parents let me choose.

"Dad and Mom came to every game I played in. They were very involved in everything I ever did and very supportive. By the time I played fullback on the Jesuit team we became state champions. I was six feet two and weighed 215, and I was fast. I did the 100-yard dash in 9.9. My second sport was track, which I really enjoyed because it was an individual's sport. Sports taught me self-discipline, how to rely on oneself, how to sacrifice for success. It has helped me greatly in business.

"It was time to choose between football and the restaurant business. I had many athletic scholarship offers, but none at schools teaching the restaurant business. I went to Mom and Dad and asked what they wanted me to do. They were so proud that I had a great athletic career. I knew they liked the idea that their son excelled, but I also knew they harbored a desire that I follow them in the restaurant business. I opted for the University of Denver School of Restaurant and Hotel Management.

"I had fallen in love with a beautiful cheerleader, Melanie Heiny, while I was at Jesuit. She was fourteen, and I was sixteen. It was the classic storybook romance. But when the time came to go to Denver I was heartsick, because I knew I would be away from her for three years. Homesick is nothing compared to heartsick. I had a great time in Denver, but I was lonely."

A D E L A : *Richard's greatest love was his German shepherd, Hobo. We got him after we were robbed at gunpoint in our home. Richard went everywhere with that dog, slept with him, bathed him, fed him. It was Richard's dog.*

We'd had him for some time when it came time for Richard to go to Denver for college. The dog moped around the house, and I could see he was just miserable without Richard. He got worse, and I took him to the vet and found he had heartworms and was dying. One day, when Richard was about to come home on holiday, the dog came to breakfast, looked at me with his sad eyes, and died.

There was no way I could bring myself to tell Richard on the phone. I took his sweetheart, Melanie, with me to pick him up at the airport and asked her to break the news to Richard.

Richard got home, went straight to his bedroom, and cried for the better part of the day. I don't think he will ever have another dog that he'll love as much as he did Hobo.

FERDIE: Figuring that his older brother had studied in Europe and he too should balance his American training with European training, Richard wanted to go to Madrid to complete his education.

"When it came time to go to Europe," Richard remembers, "the love problem got worse, for Melanie couldn't just catch a plane and come to see me in Madrid. We were desperately unhappy about the impending separation.

"In affairs of the heart there was no better professor than my dad. He took me aside as I was preparing to leave for Europe and said, 'Marry her, son. If you don't, you'll be pining away, it will make you sad and affect your studies. We'll support you.' So I did.

"Madrid was special. I found a great teacher of flamenco guitar, Pucherette. My schooling was advanced and interesting. My wife took to the easy life of the Madrileños, and my father had seen fit to encourage my education in another unusual way.

"He gave me an American Express card with instructions to visit every great restaurant in Spain whenever possible. When we left Madrid I had a head full of information and a belly full of fine food.

"I immediately immersed myself in business, working alongside my dad while Casey ran the Sarasota Columbia. It was another great education. My father allowed me to implement my new ideas.

"For example, in 1979, I decided that the Columbia Café was going to waste, so I opened a jazz club. I played bongos, jazz guitar, and conga drums with the band, and we did real well. I had had rock and roll bands in high school and college, so it wasn't anything new. And, when that was going good, I built the Warehouse, a rough-wood club behind the café. My dad didn't find out until one week before it opened. He just smiled when he found out.

"Thereafter we opened a succession of clubs, called Cha-Cha Coconuts, in Tampa's Harbour Island (1985), St. Petersburg (1988), Sand Key (1989), Sarasota (1989), and Daytona Beach (1994).

"Today I still compete in athletics. In 1990 I won a triathlon, in which you have to excel in swimming, bicycling, and running. I was thirty-seven years old at the time. The Cha-Cha Coconuts triathlon team won the state championship in 1992–93.

"In 1993 I decided to run the Los Angeles Marathon and dedicate it to my dad, who had just passed away. Marathons are grueling endurance contests, and I hate them, but that was all the more reason to force myself to honor the memory of my father. My father had died in December, and the marathon was to be held on his birthday, March 6.

"It was 107° in L.A. when I lined up to start. I had had a T-shirt made up which read 'Hail Cesar!' It was a tough fifteen-mile run, and I didn't know if I could do it, but all along the way, people who watched me pass by would begin to yell, 'Hail Cesar!' and it was as if my dad was in the crowd cheering me on. I finished the race, in honor of my father, a guy who always backed me with love and affection and who only wanted me to be the best I could be."

Richard has two daughters. Lauren is eighteen years old and the more serious of the two. She favors business over art and is already involved in the restaurant management. Andrea is sixteen and probably another Adela in the making. She is an accomplished pianist and loves to dance and act. She was the youngest ever to get the plum role of the ingenue in the school production of *Oklahoma!*

"She's the ham in the family," says a proud Richard. Perhaps, somewhere up above, Cesar is smiling. "Just like me," he is saying.

Chapter Eleven

WINE

Columbus once said at a Spanish dinner in his honor after his second trip to America, "El vino hace concebir ideas nobles" (Wine gives birth to noble ideas).

Wine's primary purpose is to give pleasure. And the wines from Spain fulfill this joyful purpose admirably. Spain, only slightly bigger in area than the state of California, has more land under vine than any other country in the world. From these vineyards come an impressive array of wines well suited to today's tastes.

Wine making is not a recent development in Spain. To appreciate the country's long, illustrious viticultural history, we look to the Phoenicians, who first came to the Iberian Peninsula in 1100 B.C. and developed a fledgling wine industry there. Then followed the Romans, who took the Spanish wine industry to a higher level by expanding the vineyards and improving wine-making techniques.

The next proponents of the art of the vine in Spain were medieval monks. Seven hundred years of Arab domination did little to hinder their ecological progress. They continued to improve wine-making and grape-growing techniques during this period in the seclusion of their monasteries.

By the fifteenth and sixteenth centuries, more than five hundred wineries were thriving in the Rueda region north of Madrid. And by the nineteenth century, brandy was being made with great zeal in Jerez and exported widely in Europe.

This steady advancement of wine making continued throughout the centuries, culminating today in a country that successfully marries age-old traditions with twentieth-century technology. Spain now boasts forty distinct, officially recognized growing regions, or denominations of origin, and makes wines ranging from complex, flavorful reds and crisp, bone-dry whites to refreshing sparkling wines, celebrated sherry, and the world's first brandy.

There is clearly something special about Spain when it comes to wine. That something is simple: its soil and climate are absolutely ideal for growing *Vitis vinifera,* the famed European wine grape species.

Depending on the location in Spain, the effect of soil and climate on grapes can vary dramatically. For instance, Rioja's clay and limestone soil yields grapes that produce full-bodied wines with deep color, while the white, chalky earth of the sherry region retains the moisture of the winter rains to sustain the ripening grapes through the hot growing season. In the Penedes, where some vineyards are planted at altitudes as high as 1,500 feet, crisp wines with a fresh fruitiness are produced.

As important as soil and climate are in influencing wine quality, the grape variety is most important in determining a wine's characteristics. As the scene of wine making for millennia, Spain has developed many native grape varieties that produce wines reflecting the characters of its many regions.

Rioja is easy to like, both as a wine and as a place. Unfolding across the valley of the Ebro River, Rioja was in the direct path of Christian pilgrims traveling to the holy site of Santiago de Compostela. The area still possesses many reminders of its fascinating history. Castles and monasteries abound, and ancient cities such as Briones and Laguardia are still thriving, much as they were in medieval days.

Rioja remained important during the Middle Ages, with monasteries being built throughout the region. In one of them—San Millan de Suso—the poet monk Gonzalo de Berceo in the thirteenth century recorded one of the first known samples of written Castilian. He was modest about his work: the closing line of one of his poems suggested that it might be worth "un vaso de bon vino" (a glass of good wine).

Rioja wine making resembles that of Bordeaux in that select grape varieties are judiciously blended to make a wine that embodies the best characteristics of each variety. In Rioja they take this one step further and marry the grapes from subregions. The denomination of origin Rioja Alavesa, with its high altitudes, moderate climate, and limestone/clay soil, produces elegant, fresh wines. Rioja Alta, also blessed with high elevation, sand, and moderate climate, is known for complex, finely structured wines. Low in altitude and flat, Rioja Baja has alluvial clay soil and produces high-alcohol, low-acid wines. Made separately, their wines can be quite different, but the winemakers frequently blend the wines made from native grapes.

In Rioja, the Tempranillo grape is star. Its qualities of good fruit flavor and relatively high tannin levels that allow the wine to age well have helped Rioja create some of the finest and best-known wines produced in Spain today. When grown in relatively cool regions like parts of Rioja, this Spanish grape produces superior red wines, which are elegant with a fresh cherry aroma when young, and smooth, complex, and velvety when aged. While red wines have placed Rioja in the ranks of the world's finest wines, the region produces some fine white wines as well, using the native grapes Viura, Garnacha Blanca, and Malvasia.

Rioja's fame is certainly well deserved, and its superiority was recognized with the award of Spain's first D.O.C. (Qualified Denomination of Origin), confirming its excellent quality and exacting standards. Every aspect of the wine-making process is overseen by the local control board, so consumers are assured that each Rioja wine meets strict standards governing grape growing, vinification, the type and quality of the grapes used, aging, bottling, and labeling of the wines.

Perhaps most unique in this region of extraordinary wines is the aging principle followed in Rioja. Of all the great red-wine-producing regions in the world, Rioja stands virtually alone in its practice of cellaring the wine until it is ready to drink. Rioja wine must spend time aging both in oak casks and in bottles. Though the regulations set strict minimum aging periods, most wineries exceed these minimums.

A Crianza wine spends a minimum of twelve months in oak cask and may not be sold until its third year. Reserva wines, produced only in years of good harvest, are not released until their fourth year and spend at least one year in oak and the rest in bottle. Gran Reserva wines are made only in years with an exceptional harvest; they are the finest Rioja has to offer, spending a minimum of two years in oak and then three years in bottle. As wines age, they become refined and elegant and gain greatly in complexity. At one time all Rioja white wines were oak-aged, just like their red counterparts. But nowadays, a number of them are cold-fermented and not oak-aged, depending on the style of the winemaker.

Rioja's fine climate enables it to continually produce delicious wines, but variations in the yearly harvest do create differences in the vintages. Though it is difficult to generalize about all Rioja wines because of their diversity in microclimate and soils, a vintage chart is still useful as a general guideline to selecting Rioja wines.

The lighter, younger red and white wines from Rioja are delightful with grilled fish, chicken, and vegetable recipes. More complex dishes, sauced meats, and the assertive flavors of lamb, beef, and game find their perfect companions in Rioja Reserves, or Gran Reservas. A valuable rule in this matching game is that a delicious Rioja wine will make any well-made dish even more enjoyable.

Luis Diaz is the expert who finds the wines for the Columbia. Luis Diaz and Cesar Gonzmart were cousins and grew up together in Cuba. When Batista fell and Castro was coming in, Luis needed desperately to leave Cuba. He asked his cousin Cesar to help him. He was penniless at the time, and Casimiro and Cesar brought him to Tampa and gave him a job starting as a busboy at the Columbia Restaurant. He worked for his cousin for ten years. He then went to work for a famous liquor company called Schieffelin and Sommerset, working there for twenty-two years. With a good reputation in the wine business, he now has his own wine company. He goes to Spain every year to select the best wines. He has been doing this for the Columbia Restaurant for three years.

Luis says, "Don Cesar Reserva 85, Red, is a marvelous wine chosen by Richard and Casey Gonzmart in honor of their father and my cousin, Cesar. The selection was a Reserva famous for its quality. An extraordinary reserva wine with deep ruby colors. Aged in oak, full-bodied with a pleasant blackberry character. Very smooth. This is Rioja with capital letters. Highly recommended with any meat dish.

"Don Cesar White 92, Rioja. This is the best white wine we found in Rioja. An exciting wine, fresh, crisp, and lively with a rich pear aroma. Concentrated

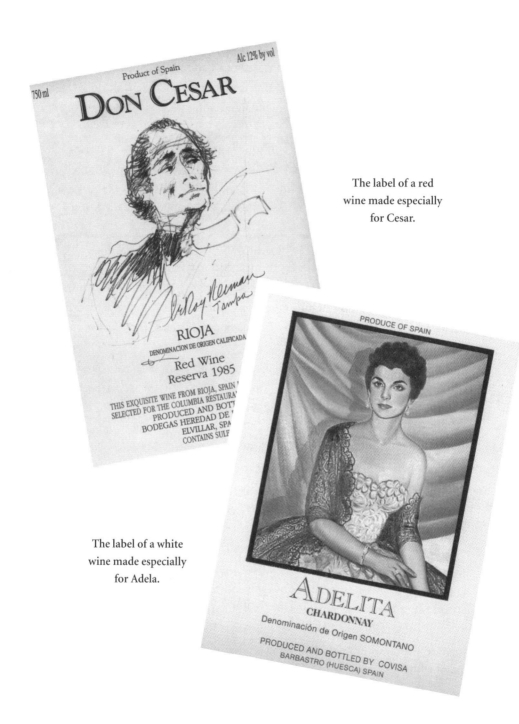

Product of Spain

Alc 12% by vol

750 ml

DON CESAR

RIOJA

DENOMINACION DE ORIGEN CALIFICADA

Red Wine
Reserva 1985

THIS EXQUISITE WINE FROM RIOJA, SPAIN
SELECTED FOR THE COLUMBIA RESTAURA
PRODUCED AND BOTT
BODEGAS HEREDAD DE
ELVILLAR, SPA
CONTAINS SULF

The label of a red
wine made especially
for Cesar.

PRODUCE OF SPAIN

ADELITA

CHARDONNAY

Denominación de Origen SOMONTANO

PRODUCED AND BOTTLED BY COVISA
BARBASTRO (HUESCA) SPAIN

The label of a white
wine made especially
for Adela.

with a rich fruity aftertaste. This wine is a wonderful accompaniment for snapper Alicante or the famous paella. It is a wonderful wine with any fish dish.

"These wines were selected especially for Cesar Gonzmart. Through his love of music and food and his remarkable ability to make them both magical and memorable, Cesar Gonzmart has kept the spirit of the Columbia alive.

"As he dined at the Columbia, LeRoy Neiman was so inspired by the performance of Cesar Gonzmart's magic violin that he sketched an animated portrait, capturing the essence of Cesar. It became the illustration on the label of his red wine.

"For Adela we traveled far and wide to look for and find the best wine to represent her. We found it in the Sierra of the Pineros close to the city of Barbastro. It is a wine from the Chardonnay grape, very rare to find in Spain. It is being made exclusively for the Columbia Restaurant. It is labeled Adelita. It is a white wine fermented in stainless steel tanks, chosen for its full flavor and light spirit. It stands as a tribute to Adelita, the wonderful woman this wine was made to honor. The late Teok Carrasco painted the portrait of her that appears on the label."

Note: Parts of the preceding material on the wines of Spain are reprinted by permission from the 1993 **Wines of Spain** *guide, written by Rory Callahan, a California-trained enologist who directs a wine program run in conjunction with New York University.*

Chapter Twelve

The Columbia Saga
Continues

FERDIE: With the death of Cesar Gonzmart, Adela has taken increasingly active control of the flagship Columbia Restaurant in Ybor City.

As usual, she is helped by faithful employees. In the tradition of Pijuan, Pete, Lola, Pepin, and Henry Tudela, these are employees who came to the Columbia to stay.

Joe Roman is a waiter who has forty-two years of service. He is surprisingly spry and energetic and still has black undyed hair. He is known as the Singing Waiter, because he hums and sings as he waits on tables. His favorite song? "I Left My Heart in San Francisco," which in his case should be "I Left My Heart in Ybor City."

If there is one man who reflects the Columbia family feeling it is the general manager, George Guito. It is virtually impossible to go to the Columbia without running into George. He is there from opening to closing.

George started out in Ybor City delivering prescriptions for my father in La Económica Drugstore. At fifteen he got a job at the Columbia as a porter.

ADELA: *Cesar, noticing the willingness of the young, eager-to-please boy, let him do odd jobs as they were needed. He proved he could fix a clogged sink and do other light plumbing. Then he proved adept at electricity and also carpentry. He was so anxious to learn that he became the star all-around Mr. Fix-it. When an emergency occurred, we called George.*

It wasn't long before Cesar let him try his hand in the kitchen. He learned cooking, and he learned to be a salad man and a sandwich man and, when no

A satisfied Casimiro II reflects on the fulfillment of his dreams and the continuation of his restaurant, 1960.

one was looking, to mix a drink. George was not above being a busboy or a waiter. George ended up doing every job at the Columbia but playing in Richard's rock and roll band.

George has been an indispensable part of the Columbia family. In 1992 we made him general manager of the Ybor City Columbia. He has applied himself with the same energy, love, and attention that he has shown in all the thirty-two years he has worked for us.

We have been extremely lucky with our employees. We like to think that they are part of our family. Our current chef, Francisco (Paco) Duarte, from Cádiz, continues in that tradition. I also feel that you don't have to be a master chef or top headwaiter or pianist to fit into our family. One such person is Lula Tollaman, who has been our ladies' room attendant for thirty-eight years. She has been a sparkling addition to our family. Quiet, courteous, and kind, she has that in common with the other members of our family.

With people such as these, is it any wonder that the Columbia is known for its friendly ambience?

FERDIE: Today the original Columbia Restaurant occupies one city block and includes eleven dining rooms, which seat up to 1,660 patrons. Five additional Columbias are located throughout Florida, each offering its own unique charm while maintaining the same high standards of quality established by the original Columbia. These restaurants are located in Harbour Island in Tampa; St. Armand's Circle in Sarasota; St. Augustine; the Pier in St. Petersburg; and Daytona Beach. We have also opened two Italian restaurants, named Mangiare Ristorante, in Clearwater Beach and Daytona Beach. Altogether the eight restaurants employ well over 1,200 people.

The Columbia Restaurant in Ybor City is the oldest restaurant in the state of Florida. Honored with a Five Forks rating by the government of Spain as the outstanding Spanish restaurant in America, it is the largest Spanish restaurant in the United States. It has been inducted into *Nation's Restaurant News* 1990 Fine Dining Hall of Fame; is the winner of the *Fortune* Magazine 1991 Epicurean Rendezvous Award for being one of the finest 100 restaurants in Florida; and is ranked seventh in *Florida Trend's* 1991 Golden Spoon Awards for the top ten restaurants in Florida.

The Columbia continues in the ninety-year tradition of excellent food in elegant surroundings. In the flagship Columbia in Ybor City, one can still eat in the fast-service hurly-burly of the coffee shop, or dine in the quiet dignity of the Fonda, as the cigar makers used to do, or choose the elegance of the Quixote, where Cesar Gonzmart started as a violinist and where Adela played the piano, or enjoy the breezy, well-lit splendor of the Patio. In the evenings, the tradition of excellent entertainment inaugurated by Cesar and Adela continues in the Siboney Room.

Dining at the Columbia continues to be an event. A sense of occasion is felt by first-time diners, for here the greats of America dined, and the presence of Babe Ruth, Lou Gehrig, and Ted Williams still lingers. The ghosts of Jack Dempsey, Gene Tunney, Primo Carnera, and Rocky Marciano are here, alongside Carmen Amaya, Sabicas, Cesar Romero, Errol Flynn, John Garfield, Harry Carey, Arthur Kennedy, Gig Young, and hundreds from the world of politics, including John F. Kennedy.

It has been an exciting, glittering, momentous place, its history a reflection of the American Dream at its best. The Columbia flagship lives on, just as Casimiro foresaw it in 1905 when he named his modest establishment "The Gem of All Spanish Restaurants."

GLOSSARY

ají: green pepper

ajiaco: Cuban creole stew

ajillo: with garlic

ajo: garlic

ajonjoli: sesame

albóndiga: meatball

alcachofa: artichoke

Alicante: province in Spain

ali-oli: garlic mayonnaise

almendra: almond

amarillo: yellow

arándano azul: blueberry

arroz: rice

asado: roast (n.); roasted (adj.)

bacalao: codfish

barbacoa: barbecue

berenjena: eggplant

bistec: steak

bizcocho: cake

blanco: white

bolita: small ball

cacerola: cooking pot or casserole dish

café: coffee

café con leche: coffee with milk

café solo: black expresso

calabaza: pumpkin, squash

calamar: squid

caldo: broth, bouillon

caldo de pollo: chicken broth

caldo de res: beef broth

callos: tripe

camarero: waiter

camarón: shrimp

cangrejo: crab

cannoli: Italian pastry filled with ricotta cheese, sugar, and candied fruits

capuchina: cloaked, hooded

carne: meat

carne con papas: meat and potatoes

castaña: chestnut

Catalan: of or from Catalonia, a region in Spain

cazuela: earthenware or metal pot

cebolla: onion

cherna: grouper

chilindrón: a spicy stew

chorizo: Spanish sausage

cochinillo: small suckling pig

cocido: stew or meal in a pot

cocina: kitchen

coco: coconut

col: cabbage

cordero: lamb

crema: cream

criollo: Creole

croqueta: croquette

cuadrito: small square

dátil: date

empanadilla: small pastry turnover with chicken or meat filling

ensalada: salad

ensaladilla: small salad

escabeche: pickled

espárrago: asparagus

especia: spice

espinaca: spinach

estofado: stewed

filete: fillet; a piece or slice of boneless meat or fish

flan: Spanish custard baked with a caramel glaze

fresco: fresh

frijol: bean

frijoles negros: black beans

frito: fried

fritura: fritter

gallego: of or from Galicia, a region in Spain

galleta: cookie or cracker

garbanzo: chickpea

guiso: stew

hígado: liver

hígado de pollo: chicken liver

huevo: egg

jaiba: crab

jamón: ham

judías verdes: green beans

langosta: lobster

leche: milk

lechón: pig

lenteja: lentil bean

macarrones: spaghetti, macaroni

madrileño: of or from Madrid

maduro: ripe

maíz: corn

malagueña: of or from Málaga, a province in Spain

malanga: taro; tropical root vegetable

mantequilla: butter

marinera: marine; of the sea

marisco: shellfish

masa: dough

melocotón: peach

membrillo: quince

mojo: a sauce of onion, garlic, and sour orange

mono: monkey

morcilla: blood sausage

ostra: oyster

pan: bread

papa: potato

pargo: red snapper

pastel: pie

patata: potato

pavo: turkey

pescado: fish

piña: pineapple

plancha: griddle

plátano: plantain

pollo: chicken

potaje: thick, rich soup

pudín: pudding

puerco: pork

puro: cigar

queso: cheese

quimbombó: okra

relleno: stuffed

Rioja: a wine-producing region in Spain

rubia: golden, blonde

rusa: Russian

salpicón: mixture

salsa: sauce

salsa de macarrones: spaghetti sauce

salteado: sautéed

sangría: sangria; red wine and fruit punch

sofrito: sauté of onions, garlic, peppers, herbs, spices, and tomatoes used as the base of many Spanish and other Latin dishes

sopa: soup

tapas: appetizers, small snacks

tocino: bacon or salt pork

tortilla: omelette

turrón: nougat candy

vaso: glass

verduras: green vegetables

viejo: old man

vino: wine

vino blanco: white wine

vino tinto: red wine

yema: yolk

yuca: cassava, yucca

ℐNDEX

Tampa WPA Symphony, 154
Tarpon Springs, 84
Tatum, Art, 100
Television, 218, 222
Tiles, 134–35; in La Fonda, 135–36; in Patio, 140; in Quixote Room, 134–36
Tollaman, Lula, 273
Tomate, Toby, 100
Tomatoes
  Catalana Sauce, 201–2
  Cuban Beef Hash, 3, 104–5
  Eggs Malagueña, 15, 21
  1905 Salad, 55
  San Isidro Salad, 54
  Spaghetti Sauce # 1, 204
  Spaghetti Sauce # 2, 204
  Spanish Cold Tomato Soup, 49
  Spanish Lobster, 131
  Stuffed Green Peppers, 212
Torrijas, 251
Torta de Guayaba y Queso, 245–46
Tortillas
  à la Española, 25
  al Ron, 15, 24
  de Camarones, 24–25
  de Coliflor, 20
  de Espárragos, Papas, y Cebollas, 19
  de Papas y Cebollas, 22–23
  de Plátanos, 23
Trafficante, Santo (father), xxii, 95
Trafficante, Santo (son), xxii
Tristano, Lenny, 100
Tropicana (Havana), 166
Tudela, Henry, xxiii, *99*, 99–100
Tuna
  Fish Basque Style, 116–17
  Russian Salad, 71
  San Isidro Salad, 54
Tunney, Gene, 274
Turkey, Roast, Cuban Style, 185–86

Turnip Greens Soup, 3, 50
Turrones, 194, 196, 198
Two Brothers Dairy, 90

University of Denver School of Restaurant and Hotel Management, 263

Valenti, Domenico, 134
Valenti, J. C., xxii
Valenti, Tony, xxii
Vegetables. *See also* Corn; Eggplant; Onions; Potatoes; Tomatoes
  appetizers
    Eggplant, Marinated Italian Style, 68
    Fried Ripe Plantains, 69
    Potatoes in Garlic Mayonnaise, 71
    Russian Salad, 71
    Spinach Balls, 75
    Stuffed Mashed Potato Balls, 75
    Water Chestnut Meatballs, 76
  egg dishes
    Cauliflower Omelette, 20
    Eggs with Vegetables, Shrimp, and Ham, 22
    Navy Bean Soup Cuban Style, 43
  entrees
    Artichokes, Stuffed, 211–12
    Chicken Sauté, 184
    Eggplant, Stuffed, 213
    Filet of Tenderloin Steak Creole à la Ferdie Pacheco, 109
    Green Peppers, Stuffed, 212
    Paella Havana, 146
    Paella Oriental, 147
    Pasta, Meatball, and Broccoli Casserole, 208
    Plantains Temptation, 211
    White Bean Torte, 213